Supporting South Asian Families
with a Child with Severe Disabilities

of related interest

Parenting in Poor Environments
Stress, Support and Coping
Deborah Ghate and Neal Hazel
ISBN 1 84310 069 X

Imprisoned Fathers and their Children
Gwyneth Boswell and Peter Wedge
ISBN 1 85302 972 6

Assessing Children's Needs and Circumstances
The Impact of the Assessment Framework
Hedy Cleaver and Steve Walker
with Pam Meadows
ISBN 1 84310 159 9

The Views and Experiences of Disabled Children
and Their Siblings
A Positive Outlook
Clare Connors and Kirsten Stalker
ISBN 1 84310 127 0

The Child's World
Assessing Children in Need
Edited by Jan Horwath
ISBN 1 85302 957 2

Meeting the Needs of Ethnic Minority Children – Including
Refugee, Black and Mixed Parentage Children
A Handbook for Professionals
Second Edition
Edited by Kedar Nath Dwivedi
ISBN 1 85302 959 9

Social Work, Immigration and Asylum
Debates, Dilemmas and Ethical Issues for Social Work
and Social Care Practice
Edited by Debra Hayes and Beth Humphries
ISBN 1 84310 194 7

Supporting South Asian Families with a Child with Severe Disabilities

Chris Hatton, Yasmeen Akram, Robina Shah,
Janet Robertson and Eric Emerson

Jessica Kingsley Publishers
London and New York

First published in the United Kingdom in 2004
by Jessica Kingsley Publishers Ltd
116 Pentonville Road
London N1 9JB, England
and
29 West 35th Street, 10th fl.
New York, NY 10001-2299, USA

www.jkp.com

Copyright © 2004 Chris Hatton, Yasmeen Akram, Robina Shah,
Janet Robertson and Eric Emerson

Library of Congress Cataloging in Publication Data
A CIP catalog record for this book is available from the Library of Congress

British Library Cataloguing in Publication Data
A CIP catalogue record for this book is available from the British Library

ISBN 1 84310 161 0

Printed and Bound in Great Britain by
Athenaeum Press, Gateshead, Tyne and Wear

Contents

List of Figures and Tables

Figures

Tables

Acknowledgements

The project was carried out at the Hester Adrian Research Centre, University of Manchester until its untimely closure, and the writing took place with the support of the Institute for Health Research, Lancaster University. We are very grateful to all the many professionals who helped put us into contact with families. We would particularly like to thank all the parents and family members who took part in the project. They spent a lot of time sharing their experiences with us, often under very difficult circumstances. We hope this book does justice to what the families told us.

This research project was commissioned by the English Department of Health as part of the Supporting Parents Research Initiative; the views expressed in this publication are those of the authors and not necessarily those of the Department of Health.

Chapter One

Introduction

The Research and Policy Context

In this book we present the findings of a research study carried out between 1998 and 2001, exploring the experiences of South Asian[1] families with a child with severe disabilities. There are two major reasons why it is important to build a rich picture of the lives of these families. First, some studies have shown that South Asian families with a person with disabilities are particularly disadvantaged in terms of housing, income, employment and health (Chamba *et al.* 1999; Hatton *et al.* 1998). Despite the high support needs of these families, South Asian families with a person with disabilities actually receive fewer benefits and support services compared to White families in similar circumstances (Chamba *et al.* 1999). Second, several policies have been developed to help families with a child with disabilities (Department of Health 1998, 1999, 2001). Although they all highlight the importance of improving services for families from minority ethnic communities, none gives clear guidance on how this could and should be done.

In our study, we wanted to build on previous studies and to produce findings that would help policy-makers plan better service supports for South Asian families with a child with severe disabilities. We also wanted to explore issues that were important to parents, in a way that put parents' voices at the heart of the study. To meet these aims, the study had three phases.

Phase 1 involved in-depth interviews with 26 South Asian families of a child with severe learning disabilities. These interviews explored parents' experiences of having a child with severe disabilities. Parents also provided guidance on what we should ask about in Phase 2, and what interview schedules we should use.

Phase 2 involved structured interviews with 136 South Asian parents of a child with severe disabilities, including reinterviewing the 26 parents who participated in Phase 1. Where possible, this survey consisted of interview schedules from previous research, so we could compare the findings of this study to previous work. Phase 2 focused on the characteristics of the family, the resources available to them, what information the family had and needed, how the disclosure of the child's disability was handled, what social support was needed and received from family, friends and services, the social life of the child with disabilities and of the family, how parents coped, and the physical health and mental health of parents.

Phase 3 involved going back to 20 of the 26 parents who had taken part in Phase 1 and Phase 2. In short interviews, parents commented on our interpretations of the Phase 1 and Phase 2 interview findings, and suggested improvements. We also asked parents to add anything important they felt was missing from the Phase 1 and Phase 2 interviews. Finally, parents were asked to reflect on the major messages of the research findings for policy and practice.

Putting the three phases together, we were interested in the following questions:

1. What are the experiences of South Asian families with a child with severe disabilities?

2. Are there differences in the experiences of particular South Asian communities?

3. What do families need from services, and what are they getting?

4. What helps families?

5. What do policy-makers and services need to do to help families?

This chapter begins by looking at research that has been published that is relevant to South Asian families with a child with severe disabilities, to review what we know about these families. It will then describe current policies relevant to South Asian families with a child with severe disabilities, highlighting that these policies should make South Asian families a high priority for better service support. The chapter will finish by describing in more detail the approach we took to the study, how we carried it out and who took part.

The rest of the book will focus on the findings of our study. Chapter 2 describes the circumstances of the families and the resources available to them. Chapter 3 outlines the characteristics of the children with disabilities involved in the study. Chapter 4 concentrates on the information available to families, from how the child's disability was disclosed to the family through to the current information needs of families. Chapter 5 describes the informal supports used by the family to help care for the child with disabilities, including support from family members within the household, family and friends outside the household, and religious organisations. Chapter 6 outlines the service supports used by families, including their views of the future for themselves and their child. Chapter 7 looks at the social life of the child with disabilities and their parents. Chapter 8 considers how parents cope, and the physical and mental health of parents. In all these chapters, findings from all three phases of the project are discussed together. Numerical information from Phase 2 is compared, where possible, to previous studies, and any differences in the experiences of families across different South Asian communities are investigated. Important themes from Phase 1 and Phase 3 interviews are highlighted by including quotes from parents; these help to bring the voices of parents centre-stage throughout the book.

Chapter 9 brings together the findings of the study, to investigate what factors are particularly important in helping families. Finally, Chapter 10 outlines the major implications of our study for policy-makers and those delivering services.

The research background

The experiences of South Asian families with a person with disabilities have, until recently, received little attention from researchers. This is surprising, as there are good reasons to think that South Asian families with a person with disabilities will have particularly high needs for service support, yet will not receive services that meet their needs as families.

Before discussing the family research it is important to place our study within the context of the experience of South Asian communities in the UK generally. The 2001 Census (Office for National Statistics 2003) reported that South Asian communities made up 4.0 per cent of the UK population (1.8% Indian, 1.3% Pakistani, 0.5% Bangladeshi, 0.4% Asian Other, according to Census categories), adding up to some 2.3 million people. As South Asian communities have proportionally more young people compared to White communities, the number of people from South Asian communities is rising and will continue to do so.

The number of South Asian people with learning disabilities in the UK is also rising substantially (Emerson and Hatton 1999), partly due to the general rise in numbers of South Asian people in the UK. There are also some studies suggesting that severe learning disabilities may be much more common among some South Asian communities compared to White communities (Emerson *et al.* 1997; Kerr 2001), although studies carried out in different parts of the UK are inconsistent (Emerson and Hatton in press; McGrother *et al.* 2002). It is certainly beyond doubt that there are now substantial and rising numbers of South Asian children with severe intellectual disabilities of school age in the UK.

It is also beyond doubt that people from South Asian communities living in the UK generally experience substantial inequalities, discrimination and disadvantage. People from South Asian communities are more likely than their White peers to live in poor housing, be unemployed, be working in semi-skilled or unskilled jobs if employed, experience poorer physical and mental health, and experience discrimination in education, health and social services (Ahmad and Atkin 1996; Modood *et al.* 1997; Nazroo 1997, 1998). Pakistani and Bangladeshi communities are particularly likely to experience such disadvantage (Modood *et al.* 1997; Nazroo 1997, 1998).

This experience of being disadvantaged is magnified for South Asian families with a person with disabilities. South Asian families with a person with learning disabilities experience disadvantage in terms of housing, employment, transport, income and benefits compared to White families with a person with learning disabilities (Chamba *et al.* 1999; Hatton *et al.* 1998), who are themselves a disadvantaged group (Beresford 1995). Many South Asian families with a person with disabilities urgently need support. For example, many South Asian families (10–19%) have more than one child with disabilities or are lone parent families (2–19%; Chamba *et al.* 1999; Hatton *et al.* 1998).

The prevailing stereotype in the UK is that people from minority ethnic groups have large and supportive extended family networks and therefore neither need nor want service support (Atkin and Rollings 1996). Studies of South Asian families with a person with disabilities have consistently nailed this stereotype as a myth. It is true that South Asian mothers of children with learning disabilities generally report high levels of practical and emotional support from partners and other children living in the household, where they are present (Chamba *et al.* 1999; Hatton *et al.* 1998). However, UK South Asian households with a person with disabilities are generally small (for example five people, Hatton *et al.* 1998). Furthermore, South Asian families with a person with learning disabilities receive less support from extended family networks compared to White families in similar circumstances

(Chamba *et al.* 1999; Hatton *et al.* 1998), largely due to family members being geographically distant.

As South Asian families are often in disadvantaged circumstances with little support from extended family or friends, it is not surprising that parents report needing support from services (Baxter *et al.* 1990; Chamba *et al.* 1999; Hatton *et al.* 1998; Mir *et al.* 2001). However, they are much less likely to receive a whole range of services at all, let alone services that meet family needs.

The first hurdle for families is getting information about the support services available. Although South Asian families report high levels of aware-ness of general health services such as the family doctor or dentist, awareness of support services for the person with disabilities such as speech therapy, psy-chology or psychiatry is much lower (Chamba *et al.* 1999; Hatton *et al.* 1998). South Asian parents repeatedly identify language and information needs as crucial if they are to access support services (Baxter *et al.* 1990; Chamba *et al.* 1999; Hatton *et al.* 1998). English language fluency seems to be crucial for getting information about available service supports. However, most South Asian parents of a person with learning disabilities do not speak, read or write English (Baxter *et al.* 1990; Chamba *et al.* 1999; Hatton *et al.* 1998).

Researchers have consistently reported low use among South Asian families of a range of family support services such as short-term breaks for families and family support groups (Chamba *et al.* 1999; Mir *et al.* 2001). Where service supports are provided, they rarely meet the language, cultural and religious needs of the person with learning disabilities or of the family (Azmi *et al.* 1997; Chamba *et al.* 1999; Hatton *et al.* 1998; Shah 1995). This sometimes leads to parents withdrawing their child from particularly poor services.

Caring for a person with disabilities in such circumstances takes its physical and mental toll on parents. South Asian parents of a person with learning disabilities report high frequencies of visits to GPs and hospitals for their own health needs and extremely high rates of distress indicative of a mental health problem (Hatton *et al.* 1998). The two factors most strongly associated with distress among South Asian parents were lower household income and caring for more than one person with learning disabilities (Hatton *et al.* 1998).

A number of researchers have asked South Asian parents themselves how services could be improved. They consistently report similar priorities: raising parental awareness by increasing the linguistic competence of services;

employing more South Asian staff throughout mainstream services; ensuring that mainstream services routinely meet the language, cultural and religious needs of people with learning disabilities; providing families with a reliable keyworker; building support groups for South Asian parents; and improving the material circumstances of families (Baxter *et al.* 1990; Chamba *et al.* 1999; Hatton *et al.* 1998; Mir *et al.* 2001).

Researchers have been reporting the circumstances and needs of South Asian families with a person with disabilities for over a decade, with little evidence of improvements in services over time. Do current policies give families hope that things will get better?

The policy background

Children with disabilities and their families have historically been excluded from policies aimed at improving the lives of children generally (Connors and Stalker 2003). However, several recent policies have highlighted the importance of improving services for children with disabilities and their families. Three recent policy initiatives have particular relevance for South Asian families with a child with severe disabilities. The National Carers Strategy (Department of Health 1999) is designed to help family carers in a wide range of circumstances, including parents of children with disabilities. Quality Protects (Department of Health 1998) is designed to improve services for children, with children with disabilities highlighted as a priority group. Valuing People (Department of Health 2001) is designed mainly to improve services for adults with learning disabilities, although there are also some policies about improving services for children with learning disabilities. These policy initiatives will be briefly discussed in turn.

The National Carers Strategy

The central aim of the National Carers Strategy (Department of Health 1999) is to improve the quality of life of family carers by:

1. Giving carers the freedom to have a life of their own.

2. Giving carers time for themselves.

3. Giving carers the opportunity to work, if that is what they want to do.

4. Giving carers control over their life and over the support they need in it.

5.   Improving the health and well-being of carers.

6.   Encouraging carers' integration into the community.

7.   Giving carers peace of mind.

According to the Strategy, these ambitious aims are to be achieved through three strategies: information, support and care.

1.   Information

    (a)   A new charter on what people can expect from long-term care services and setting new standards.

    (b)   Considering how to improve the consistency of charging for services.

    (c)   Carers need good health information.

    (d)   NHS Direct helpline for carer information.

    (e)   Government information on the internet.

2.   Support

    (a)   Carers need to be involved in planning and providing services.

    (b)   Local caring organisations should be consulted.

    (c)   Comment cards, advice surgeries, carers' weeks are good ways to involve carers.

3.   Care

    (a)   Carers' rights to have their own health needs met.

    (b)   New powers for local authorities to provide services for carers, as well as for those being cared for.

    (b)   First focus of the new powers should be on helping carers take a break.

    (d)   New special grant to help carers take a break.

Research with South Asian families with a person with disabilities suggests that these families should be a high priority for the National Carers Strategy, although the particular strategies adopted may be of questionable relevance to South Asian families. Our study in this book explores in detail the experiences of family carers relevant to the aims of the Strategy, including the social lives of parents, employment issues, control over the services families use, and the health and well-being of parents. It also explores parents' ideas about how their lives can be improved, including ideas about information, support and care.

Quality Protects

The Quality Protects initiative is concerned with services for children, including children with disabilities (see Department of Health 1998). The Quality Protects initiative specifies several objectives for children's services, of which the following are particularly relevant to South Asian families with a child with severe disabilities.

- Objective 3. To ensure that children in need gain maximum life chance benefits from educational opportunities and health care.

- Objective 6. To ensure that children with specific social needs arising out of disability or a health condition are living in families or other appropriate settings in the community where their assessed needs are adequately met and reviewed.

- Objective 7. To ensure that referral and assessment processes discriminate effectively between different types and levels of need and produce a timely service response.

- Objective 8. To actively involve users and carers in planning services and in tailoring individual packages of care; and to ensure effective mechanisms are in place to handle complaints.

- Objective 11. To maximise the benefit to service users from the resources available, and to demonstrate the effectiveness and value for money of the care and support provided, and allow for choice and different responses for different needs and circumstances.

Once again, research that has been published suggests that South Asian families with a child with severe disabilities should be a priority group under Quality Protects. Our study investigates several issues relevant to Quality Protects, including the education that the children with disabilities receive and how child and family needs are assessed and met by support services. Parents' opinions about improving assessment procedures, education and family support services are also highlighted.

Valuing People

Finally, the White Paper *Valuing People* (Department of Health 2001) outlines a strategy for improving services primarily for adults with learning disabilities, although there are again objectives relevant to South Asian families with a child with learning disabilities. There is considerable overlap between the Valuing People strategy and the objectives of Quality Protects.

- Objective 1. To ensure that disabled children gain maximum life chance benefits from educational opportunities, health care and social care, while living with their families or other appropriate settings in the community where their assessed needs are adequately met and reviewed.

- Objective 2. As young people with learning disabilities move into adulthood, to ensure continuity of care and support for the young person and their family, and to provide equality of opportunity in order to enable as many young people as possible to participate in education, training or employment.

- Objective 4. To increase the help and support carers receive from all local agencies in order to fulfil their family and caring roles effectively.

- Objective 7. To enable people with learning disabilities to lead full and purposeful lives within their community and to develop a range of friendships, activities and relationships.

- Objective 9. To ensure that all agencies commission and provide high quality, evidence-based, and continuously improving services which promote both good outcomes and best value.

Research that has been published so far suggests that support services for South Asian families with a person with disabilities have not been high quality or evidence-based, and have not shown continuous improvements over time. Our study explores several issues relevant to Valuing People objectives. In particular it explores the social lives of the children with disabilities and, for parents of older children, the process of transition from education services to services for adults, and their plans, hopes and fears for the future.

Our study

As we have seen, some research has been published about the circumstances and needs of South Asian families with a person with disabilities, and how services respond to those needs. However, there are still substantial gaps in our knowledge base, especially when it comes to South Asian families with a child with severe disabilities. In our study we tried to address some of these gaps, using approaches that tried to overcome some of the limitations of previous work in the following ways.

First, our study involved a relatively large number of 136 families drawn from five local authority areas in England, designed to produce an ethnically diverse sample in terms of Indian, Pakistani and Bangladeshi families.

Second, the in-depth interviews in Phase 1 and Phase 3 were comprehensive and flexible, empowering parents to talk about important issues for them and enabling parents to guide the content of Phase 2 of the project. Phase 3 interviews were also used to check with parents that our interpretations of the findings made sense to them.

Third, all structured interviews in Phase 2 were translated using recognised cross-cultural translation and back-translation methods. This allowed all interviews to be conducted in the preferred language of the parents, without the need for reading or writing skills on the part of parents.

Fourth, the topic areas covered in the study were more comprehensive and wide-ranging than previous research. In addition to topics covered in previous research, information was collected on the ethnic identity of parents, the social life of the child with disabilities, the process of disclosure of the child's disability, parental coping strategies, parental anxiety and depression, various aspects of parental physical health, and the future plans of families. Areas covered in greater depth than in previous studies included aspects of the characteristics of the child with disabilities, support from services and support from family, friends and religious organisations.

Finally, where possible, interview schedules for Phase 2 were chosen where recent comparative information was available, either on South Asian families with a child with severe disabilities, South Asian adults generally, or White parents of children with learning disabilities. This enabled us to put the findings of the study into a broader context.

The families

We asked for families in five English local education authority areas in the West Midlands, North West and Yorkshire to take part in our study, through the following services:

1.   Nine schools for children with severe learning difficulties, covering the full school age range (5 to 19 years).

2.   One assessment centre for pre-school children with disabilities.

3.   One community-based service for children with special needs.

4.   One independent sector support service for ethnic minority families with a child with disabilities.

5.   One city-wide database of children receiving special education.

In all local authority areas ethical approval was obtained to carry out our study. All initial contacts with families were made by a professional working within the service, and were made in the first language of the family. We asked for consent from parents to take part in the study in different ways across different services, including:

1.   Letters being sent from the service, enclosing an information sheet concerning the research project, a reply slip and a stamped addressed envelope.

2.   Initial contact being made by a South Asian linkworker who knew the service and the family, through a phone call or a home visit, with an information sheet being sent to the family or left with the family.

3.   Invitations from service professionals to attend a parent group to discuss the research project with the research team.

Due to data protection issues we do not know how many parents declined to take part in our study, although participating services reported generally high levels of enthusiasm from parents.

Twenty-six South Asian families took part in Phase 1 and 136 South Asian families took part in Phase 2 (see Table 1.1 for details). Of these 136 families, 24 were families who had also participated in Phase 1 (one family had moved and in one family the child had died). In Phase 3, 20 of the 26 families from Phase 1 were reinterviewed (a further one family could not be contacted, and in three further families the child had died). In each family, we interviewed the person identified by the family as the main carer of the child with disabilities. The characteristics of the main carers and their families will be discussed in detail in Chapter 2.

Table 1.1 Characteristics of families taking part in Phase 1 and Phase 2		
	Phase 1	**Phase 2**
Total number of interviews	26	136
Family member interviewed		
Mother	19 (73.1%)	123 (90.4%)
Father	1 (3.8%)	11 (8.1%)
Both parents	5 (19.2%)	
Mother and sister-in-law	1 (3.8%)	
Sister		2 (1.5%)
Single parent family	2 (7.7%)	16 (11.8%)
Average age of main carer (years)	36.5 (23–51)	39.3 (20–74)
Ethnic origin of main carer		
Pakistan	24 (92.3%)	95 (69.9%)
Bangladesh	2 (7.7%)	15 (11.0%)
India		23 (16.9%)
East African Asian		3 (2.2%)
First language of main carer		
Urdu	4 (15.4%)	42 (30.9%)
Punjabi	15 (57.7%)	39 (28.7%)
Pashtu	3 (11.5%)	8 (5.9%)
Bengali	2 (7.7%)	15 (11.0%)
Hindi		5 (3.7%)
Gujerati		19 (14.0%)
Swahili		2 (1.5%)
English	2 (7.7%)	4 (2.9%)
Main carer can speak English	11 (42.3%)	60 (44.1%)
Average age of child with disabilities (years)	11.1 (2–19)	11.5 (1–21)

Child gender		
Female	12 (46.2%)	61 (44.9%)
Male	14 (53.8%)	75 (55.1%)
Number of children with disabilities		
1	20 (76.9%)	108 (79.4%)
2	4 (14.6%)	21 (15.4%)
3	1 (3.8%)	7 (5.1%)
4	1 (3.8%)	
Average number of people in household (including child with disabilities)	6.3 (3–12)	4.6 (2–10)

Phase 1 interviews

The Phase 1 interviews had two major aims. The first was to conduct an in-depth interview about parents' experiences of caring for a child with severe learning disabilities. The second aim was to guide the development of the interview schedules used in the Phase 2 interviews. Here, we asked parents to comment on which topics should be included in the Phase 2 interviews, which interview schedules were best for answering these topics, and whether the translations of the interview schedules were acceptable and made sense.

For Phase 1, a loosely structured interview schedule was developed on the basis of good practice in research interviewing (Mason 1996), important themes that had emerged in previous studies (for example Baxter *et al.* 1990; Chamba *et al.* 1999; Hatton *et al.* 1998), and discussion with experienced researchers and professionals supporting South Asian parents with a child with disabilities. The interview schedule consisted of a number of potential probe questions, although interviews were carried out flexibly to allow parents to discuss issues of importance to them that were not included in the original interview schedule. Areas covered by the Phase 1 interview schedule included the following (full details of the probe questions are given in Appendix 1):

1. Basic characteristics of the parent, child with disabilities and the family.

2. How the family found out about the child's disability, and how they reacted.

3.   Typical family life, including family activities and social life.

4.   Education and other services used by the child and the family.

5.   Support from family (both within and outside the household), friends and other non-service sources.

6.   Hope, fears, plans and dreams for the future.

7.   What would make life better for the family.

All parents were interviewed in their preferred language in their homes by the same interviewer, at a date and time of their choosing, with interviews taking around 90 minutes. All interviews were audio-recorded and transcribed into English by the interviewer or another bilingual member of the research team.

Phase 2 interviews

The Phase 2 interview was designed to produce numerical information that could be analysed statistically on a wide range of issues that were important to families. As far as possible, specific interview schedules were selected according to the following criteria:

1.   Investigating important issues according to previous research and theory and the views of parents in Phase 1 interviews.

2.   Could be translated into four languages (Urdu, Hindi, Bengali, Gujerati).

3.   Previous use in research with UK South Asian families with a person with disabilities, UK South Asian adults generally, or families with a person with disabilities.

4.   Some research evidence concerning the reliability and/or validity of the schedule.

5.   Acceptability to South Asian parents, assessed in Phase 1.

6.   As short as possible.

Where translated versions of the interview schedules were not available, they were first of all translated from English into Urdu, Hindi, Bengali and Gujerati. They were then back-translated into English by an independent translator to check that the translations made sense. The Phase 2 interview schedule asked questions about a wide range of topics, including the following (full details of the specific interview schedules used are given in Appendix 2):

1. Characteristics of the main carer, the family and the household.

2. Characteristics of the child with severe learning disabilities.

3. The social life of the child and the family.

4. How parents found out about the child's disability through the disclosure process.

5. Support from services, including parental awareness and use of a wide range of services and parents' experiences of specific services, including education, short-term care, interpreters, keyworkers and parent groups.

6. Informal (non-service) support from family, friends and others.

7. Family decision-making.

8. How parents cope.

9. Parents' mental health and physical health.

All parents were interviewed in their preferred language in their homes, at a date and time of their choosing. Interviews took on average two hours to complete, and were conducted in two parts if requested. All interviews were coded directly on to bilingual structured interview schedules. Most of the interviews were conducted by the same interviewer as the Phase 1 and Phase 3 interviews, with a team of interviewers being recruited and trained by the research team to cover the range of preferred languages.

Phase 3 interviews

The loosely structured Phase 3 interviews had two main aims. The first was to check out with parents our interpretations of the findings of our study, to see whether our interpretations were accurate, and to give more information where our interpretations had missed important issues. Parents were also asked to reflect on the major messages of the research findings for policy and practice. As with the Phase 1 interviews, a set of potential probe questions was used to guide the interviews, although interviews were again conducted flexibly. Details of the probe questions used in the Phase 3 interviews are given in Appendix 3.

All Phase 3 interviews were carried out in the same way as Phase 1 interviews, although they were shorter (around 30 minutes).

Analysis

As information from all three phases of the study will be combined throughout the book, we will briefly describe here how we analysed the information we obtained.

Phase 1 and Phase 3 interviews

As mentioned above, the 26 Phase 1 interviews were audio-recorded, transcribed and translated into English. These English-language transcripts were analysed using a qualitative approach called interpretative phenomenological analysis (IPA) (Smith 1995, 1996; Smith, Jarman and Osborn 1999). In brief, IPA, in common with many other qualitative approaches, aims to 'explore in detail the participant's view of the topic under investigation' (Smith *et al.* 1999, p.218). It does this partly through the use of loosely structured interviews, which allow the person to talk about what they feel is important rather than being constrained by the interviewer's ideas about what should be important. When interview transcripts are analysed, IPA uses the person's own words to build up a rich picture of the person's experience that the person would recognise and agree with, rather than imposing the views of the researcher on what the transcripts mean.

In our study, the main analyst of the Phase 1 interview transcripts was also the Phase 1 interviewer. The first transcript was read several times, with the analyst making notes in the left-hand margin of the transcript on comments which seemed interesting or significant. Next, potential themes relating to individual comments were made in the right-hand margin. Potential themes for the entire transcript were examined, and possible connections between themes were also noted.

This process was repeated with the second interview transcript. Themes across the two transcripts were compared and contrasted and a revised set of themes developed, by checking back through both transcripts. This process was continued for the first seven transcripts. At this point two transcripts were read by two other members of the research team, using the IPA approach. Potential themes noted by the three members of the research team were discussed, with any differences or inconsistencies resolved through the production of a revised set of themes.

IPA analysis continued, with regular discussions among members of the research team, until all 26 interviews were analysed. A set of major themes was identified, each broken down into sub-themes where relevant. A detailed report concerning the Phase 1 findings was produced, summarising each theme and sub-theme and providing supporting evidence from interview transcripts. Possible connections between themes were also identified.

The 20 Phase 3 interviews were considerably shorter than Phase 1 interviews, and were structured according to the themes identified in the IPA of the Phase 1 interviews and the major statistical findings of the first 95 Phase 2 interviews. Transcripts of Phase 3 interviews were examined for evidence of new themes or contradictions with existing themes. Only minor changes were required for a small number of sub-themes.

Phase 2 interviews

Responses from all Phase 2 interview schedule items were coded into the Statistical Package for Social Scientists (SPSS) version 10 for statistical analysis. Responses to open-ended questions were listed and coded into numerical categories by two members of the research team. A random sample of ten interview schedules was checked against SPSS codes to ensure correct coding, and all SPSS data were checked for inconsistencies and obvious coding errors.

Factor analyses were conducted where necessary to derive subscales from measures (see Hatton *et al.* 2002, for details), a particularly important process where previous research using measures had not produced subscales or had produced subscales using very different groups (for example White English-speaking parents). Descriptive statistics on all variables were conducted, and where possible comparisons were made with previous research studies using the same measures.

Depending on the nature of the data, statistical tests were used to compare different groups (for example, families from different ethnic groups), and to examine associations between variables (for example, between household income and parental health). More complex statistical analyses examined which factors were most strongly associated with a limited number of important outcome variables. These analyses are described in more detail in Chapter 9.

Note

1   In this report, 'South Asian' is used to refer to populations originating from India, Pakistan, Bangladesh, and mainly Indian families who had lived in Africa for a substantial period of time, consistent with the Policy Studies Institute 4th National Survey (Modood *et al.* 1997).

Chapter Two

The Families

This chapter describes the circumstances of the families who took part in our study. After describing the characteristics of the main carers and their families, the chapter focuses on the resources that families have available to them, including the home, transport, employment, income and benefits, and financial issues associated with caring for a child with severe learning disabilities. As almost all the main carers were parents of the child with severe intellectual disabilities, the term 'parent' rather than 'carer' will be used throughout, especially as most parents did not like the term 'carer'.

The parents

As we mentioned in Chapter 1, all our interviews were with people identified as the main carer of the child with disabilities (some characteristics of these main carers are shown in Table 1.1).

Most of the main carers who took part in our study were mothers (although a minority of these mothers reported that both parents shared the care of the child equally). This is consistent with previous UK research with families of a child with disabilities across all ethnic groups (Beresford 1995; Chamba *et al.* 1999).

The ethnicity of the families involved in our study was varied; in Phase 2 interviews most families were Pakistani (69.9%), although there were also substantial numbers of Bangladeshi (11%) and Indian (16.9%) interviewees, with the ethnicity of both parents almost invariably the same. However, families were less diverse in terms of religion. The vast majority of families were Muslim (93.4%), the remainder being Hindu (3.7%) or Sikh (2.9%).

This sample contains a smaller proportion of people of Indian ethnic origin compared to 2001 Census figures (Office for National Statistics 2003), a result of the particular areas in which our study took place. Because specific communities of immigrants tend to cluster together in specific geographic areas (Owen 1996), in our study different local authority areas had very different ethnic and religious population profiles. This means that any differences between ethnic groups found in our study must be treated cautiously, as these differences might reflect differences in services between local authority areas rather than ethnic differences.

We also asked two questions from the 4th PSI National Survey (Modood *et al.* 1997) concerning the extent to which parents felt themselves to be British and Asian (or the word they used to describe their ethnic group). As there were no differences between the parents across ethnic groups in our study, Figure 2.1 shows the results for all the parents in our study compared to the 4th PSI National Survey. As in the 4th National Survey, the vast majority of parents in our study saw themselves as Asian, although compared to the 4th National Survey fewer parents saw themselves as British and more were neutral. This may be related to the fact that only 9.2 per cent of interviewees were born in the UK, although interviewees not born in the UK had spent on average 20 years in the UK (range 1–40 years).

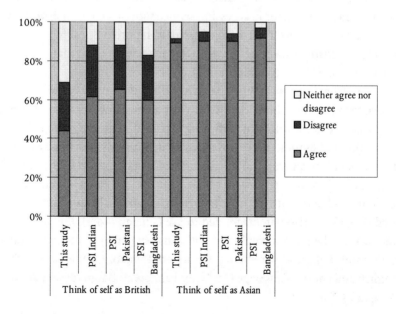

Figure 2.1 Perceived British and Asian identity: our study versus 4th PSI National Survey

In terms of marital status, 88.2 per cent of main carers interviewed in Phase 2 were in two-parent families. Single parent families (11.8%) included families where the parent was separated from the spouse (6.6%), widowed (3.7%) and single (1.5%). In UK studies, proportions of single parent South Asian families with a person with disabilities have ranged from 2 per cent to 19 per cent (Chamba *et al.* 1999; Hatton *et al.* 1998). These figures are generally lower than those of White UK families with a child with disabilities (for example 28%) (Beresford 1995) but higher than UK figures for South Asian families generally (for example 8%) (Modood *et al.* 1997). A Phase 1 parent described the isolation involved in being a single parent with a child with disabilities.

> I find it more and more difficult as he gets older because you're desperate to want your own life…as far as relationships are concerned I can't even interest myself any more. It's like I've narrowed my life down…other than me and them [one son with disabilities and one daughter without disabilities] seven days a week there is nothing and it's pretty sad. And it's lonely and it does get very difficult because you don't have anyone to turn to.
>
> *Shahina*

Previous research in the USA and the UK involving ethnic minority families with a person with learning disabilities has highlighted English language fluency as a crucial factor in accessing service supports (Hatton 2002). Among Phase 2 parents, less than half of parents reported speaking, reading or writing English, a level of English fluency lower than that reported by Chamba *et al.* (1999) (see Figure 2.2).

As in Chamba *et al.* (1999), patterns of language use were unsurprisingly associated with the ethnic identity of the parent. However, some patterns of language use were different, reflecting the different geographical areas in which the studies took place. For example, in our study Indian parents mainly used Gujerati, compared to Punjabi in the Chamba *et al.* (1999) study; Pakistanis in both studies tended to speak Urdu and/or Punjabi, but were more likely to read and write in Urdu; and Bangladeshis in both studies almost all used Bengali. Indian parents tended to use Gujerati (44%), Punjabi (17%), or one of these languages combined with English (26%) to communicate with their child; Pakistani parents tended to use Punjabi (38%), Urdu (20%), or English and another language (25%); and almost all Bangladeshi parents used Bengali (87%).

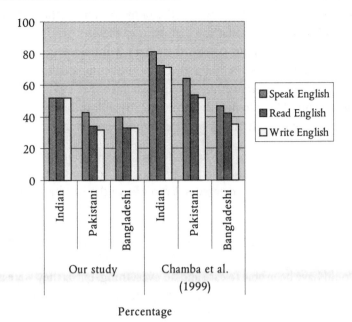

Figure 2.2 Parental English language fluency: our study versus Chamba et al. (1999)

Overall, three conclusions can be drawn about language use by South Asian parents of a child with severe disabilities:

1. English is not the preferred language of many South Asian carers of a child with severe learning disabilities.

2. There is substantial diversity of language use across ethnic groups within the UK. There is also substantial diversity of language use within ethnic groups across different geographical areas of the UK.

3. Spoken language fluency is more common than reading or written language fluency.

The household and the home

The household

In the UK population generally, household numbers are slightly higher for South Asian households (average 3.9 to 5.7 people) than for White households (average 1.4 people) (Modood *et al.* 1997). Parents in Phase 2 of our study reported a generally small household size given that this study was selecting for households with at least one child (average 4.6 people including the child with disabilities). However, the range of household sizes was very wide (2 to 10 people), similar to Chamba *et al.* (1999).

Among families taking part in the Phase 2 interviews, 21 per cent of families had more than one child with a disability, compared to 10 per cent of UK families across different ethnic groups (Chamba *et al.* 1999) and 5 per cent of largely White UK parents (Beresford 1995). Phase 1 parents with more than one child with a disability reported more demanding caring roles.

> ...especially as they [disabled son and daughter] are growing up the responsibilities increase and there is no help from anywhere. If I have to go somewhere in an emergency I can't leave the children with anyone.
>
> *Zora*

> Day by day it was getting more difficult as the children were increasing and the problem is the same. If I had one child I could have managed. I would have been able to care and do everything, but as they were increasing and time was going by and my pain was increasing. So everything became difficult.
>
> *Farida*

Housing

As with the general UK South Asian population (Modood *et al.* 1997) most of the families in Phase 2 owned their own home (56.8%), with other families renting from the local council or housing association (19.7%), renting from a private landlord (9.8%) or living with grandparents of the child with severe learning disabilities (13.6%). However, home ownership does not necessarily imply housing suitable for the care of a child with severe learning disabilities. In the Phase 2 interviews, 53 per cent of parents reported that their home was unsuitable for looking after a child with severe disabilities. This figure is similar to UK ethnic minority families (60%) (Chamba *et al.* 1999) and higher than UK White families (40%) (Beresford 1995), although these comparisons could not be tested statistically. As with Chamba *et al.* (1999), Bangladeshi parents generally reported the most housing problems, followed by Pakistani parents then Indian parents.

Parents reported a range of housing problems, which can be compared to those reported by Chamba *et al.* (1999) (see Table 2.1). Overall, parents most frequently reported problems with a lack of space in the home, the home not having enough rooms and concerns about the home being unsafe. However, fewer parents in our study compared to those in the Chamba *et al.* (1999)

Housing problem	Our study			Chamba et al. (1999)		
	Indian (%)	Pakistani (%)	Bangladeshi (%)	Indian (%)	Pakistani (%)	Bangladeshi (%)
Not enough play space	30	35	60	48	60	69
Not enough room for equipment	26	39	40	49	58	62
Not enough bedrooms	26	35	53	45	50	62
No safe/suitable garden	17	26	47	35	45	44
Difficult stairs	30	26	20	31	35	29
No downstairs toilet	22	27	27	28	43	27
No downstairs bedroom for child	26	33	33	33	42	24
House unsafe in some way	32	30	27	23	25	22
Cold	26	22	40	17	32	31
Damp	22	12	47	13	25	31
Doorways too narrow	30	13	20	13	11	9
Other	17	25	27	15	9	13

Table 2.1 Type and percentage of housing problems reported by families: our study and comparison data from Chamba et al. (1999)

study reported housing problems such as lack of space for play and equipment and lack of bedrooms, and more parents reported problems such as the house being unsafe. Overall, 29 per cent of Phase 2 parents reported that their home had been altered for their child's needs or was in the process of being altered, a similar level to that reported in Chamba et al. (1999).

Parents in Phase 1 and Phase 3 emphasised the importance of housing when caring for their child with disabilities. Unsuitable housing was often associated with inadequate income and a lack of support from services. In addition, adaptations to homes offered by local services did not always meet the cultural needs of the family.

> I think this house is far too small. I applied before I went to Bangladesh...and I've been put on a waiting list for two years. I've told them that I've got problems, especially with Ali. I really want a bigger house. I'm not getting any sort of support really. I want a kitchen and bathroom downstairs for Ali. We need a separate room for Ali.
>
> *Arslan*

> It's very hard to push [social services] to get us a house somewhere else. Like I'm not getting through to them in any way. It's very hard to stay in this small little bungalow... Like he's growing now and he's got very different and big things, like he's got a stander where I have to put him in for like sessions during the day. He's got this chair...he's got a mobility chair and it's all over scattered around the house... At the minute it's very hard to live in this place, with the other children as well.
>
> *Amani*

> Now these girls they are grown up. They need a room of their own. My big son [first child with disabilities] sleeps in a separate room. The young one [second child with disabilities] and myself can sleep in one room. I need a three-bedroom house with plenty of space downstairs. I have children's chairs etc., for which there is no room. It should be downstairs... I need a special bathroom where I can take him straight in a wheelchair, so that I can give him a bath without any difficulty. At the moment the bathroom is upstairs and it's difficult for me to carry him upstairs for a bath. The toilet is upstairs...and he [second child with disabilities] stays downstairs. The stairs are very steep so it's difficult to get up... I have been put a long way down the waiting list. I have a lot of problems... At present there is no solution in sight.
>
> *Samaya*

> Our financial situation is very bad. This is my parents' house and it needs a lot of repairs. We don't have a car either... If we had our own house then we would not have to worry what she [child with disabilities] might do to things.
>
> *Halima*

Sometimes Tahir gets up at two or five o'clock in the morning. He also hits his siblings causing distressing injuries. We need an open space or a separate room to protect the other children.

Zakiya

They [social services] also said that they would convert the living room into a kitchen. So what was the point of buying a big house? It will just be ruined. When friends or relatives come to visit the men sit separately in our culture. If we don't have a living room and a front guest room then it will cause too many problems. It is just not the practice in Asian families for men and women to sit in one room. We have spoken to the social services many times.

Faiza

Transport

Transport was often a problem for families. Although most families in the Phase 2 interviews used a family car to go out with their child (63%), only 43 per cent of main carers could drive and were thus dependent on partners for transport. Almost half the families (41%) used taxis, although this was expensive, and 13 per cent of families used lifts from family or friends. Relatively few families used public transport such as buses (15%), trains (4%) or trams (2%), to go out with their child. Compared to families from minority ethnic communities in the Chamba *et al.* (1999) study more families had cars but fewer used public transport. Similarly to Chamba *et al.* (1999), Indian and Pakistani families were more likely to have use of a family car than Bangladeshi parents. Transport was mentioned as a problem by many parents in the Phase 1 and Phase 3 interviews.

We need more transport help, as I now have three disabled girls and they have many hospital appointments. One of them is a very young baby and I cannot drive.

Azra

Household finances

Family income

As in previous surveys of families with a child with severe disabilities (Beresford 1995; Chamba *et al.* 1999), family income was low, with most families in the Phase 2 interviews reporting incomes of less than £200 per week. Again consistent with previous studies, single parent families reported lower incomes than two-parent families. Among single parent families, 27 per cent had a weekly income of less than £100 per week, 40 per cent had an income between £100 and £200, 33 per cent had an income between £200 and £300, and none had a weekly income above £300 (compared to 2%, 48%, 37% and 13% respectively for two-parent households). Incomes for single parent families in this study were lower than for South Asian single parent families with a child without disabilities (Modood *et al.* 1997) and for UK single parents generally (average weekly gross UK household income for lone parents: with one child £211; with two children £225; Office for National Statistics 2001).

Two-parent families also reported substantially lower incomes than UK two-parent families generally (average weekly gross UK household income for two parents: with one child £647; with two children £696; with three children £637; with four or more children £562; Office for National Statistics 2001).

Employment

Consistent with previous studies of families with a child with disabilities (Chamba *et al.* 1999), 91.2 per cent of mothers interviewed and 81.8 per cent of fathers interviewed in Phase 2 cared for the family full time, with most other interviewees working part time. Unlike the parents surveyed by Chamba *et al.* (1999), parents in our study were largely happy with their current employment status (86.3% of mothers; 70% of fathers) and did not consider their employment prospects to have been affected by the birth of their child with disabilities (81.4% of mothers; 40% of fathers). However, this must be set against prevailing patterns of high unemployment among UK South Asian communities, particularly among Pakistani and Bangladeshi communities (Modood *et al.* 1997) who make up the bulk of the Phase 2 parents. Indeed, for most families in our study (54.5%) there was no one in full-time employment in the household.

Child-related financial issues

It is clear that most South Asian families with a child with severe disabilities experience unsuitable housing, low income and unemployment. Do these families receive benefits to help them cover the extra costs of raising a child or children with severe learning disabilities? Previous UK studies suggest that disadvantaged families, including a disproportionate number of families in minority ethnic groups, are less likely to apply for and receive benefits for their child with disabilities (Chamba *et al*. 1999; Roberts and Lawton 1998). In our study, substantial proportions of families were not receiving benefits. The benefit with the greatest uptake was the Care Needs Allowance, received by 82.2 per cent of families (although only 52.6% of families received this at the higher rate). The Invalid Care Allowance was received by 61.5 per cent of families, and the Mobility Needs Allowance was received by only 57.9 per cent of families (30.8% at the higher rate). Although comparisons are not possible with previous studies, it is clear that there are many families eligible for benefits who are not receiving them.

As in Chamba *et al*. (1999), a number of Phase 1 parents reported difficulties and delays in getting benefits, often because parents were not aware of their existence.

> I never had any help from the health visitor… There are a lot of benefits which I could have claimed for this child which I never did because nobody informed me, not the health visitors, not the hospitals, nobody.
>
> *Jabir*

> They did not tell us [about the child's disability]. When she was 5 years old they started to pay us benefit. When she was 5 they said 'She may walk. She may not walk'. We were not happy because she is dependent. She cannot feed herself, cannot walk or speak. She is dependent on us for everything.
>
> *Seema*

> She was about 3 or 4 years old. We didn't know we could claim. Someone came from the pre-school unit, they told us to claim.
>
> *Azra*

When received, benefits are an invaluable source of financial support to families, with parents seeing benefit income very much as belonging to the child. However, even if families are in receipt of benefits, in the absence of support services and other substantial sources of income, benefits are insufficient to pay for the additional supports necessary.

> As you know there is a lot of expense on these children. If I wasn't receiving any money…I wouldn't be able to support these children well…for example Bilal's school trip for me to manage on my husband's wage would be very hard.
>
> *Zareena*

The biggest help was the financial side of it, from the money I get for Parveen... Before everything was paid for from my husband's income. The family's needs increased so we could not afford anything. Now I use Parveen's money entirely for her things. She has her own account where her money is paid in and I withdraw what I need. This way she is not dependent on us... She is very cheerful. Whatever she wants her needs are met. She is happy.

Ayesha

I mean if you want to take him [child with disabilities] out you're all right you know [with financial support from benefits]. You can buy him his videos because that's his money or take him out for days and stuff like that, but at the end of the day, like I mean I phoned up a private agency because he's got to the stage where I'm tired and I know I've got no help and I have to pay for it... And do you know how much they want for day care over the school holidays? £35 to £40 a day. Now I'm not even bringing that money home and Yusuf's money is not going to cover it.

Shahina

Benefits are crucial if the extra costs of caring for a child with severe disabilities are to be borne by the family. Previous studies have repeatedly shown the range of extra costs associated with caring for a child with severe disabilities for families across all ethnic groups (Beresford 1995; Chamba *et al.* 1999). As there were no differences between ethnic groups in our study concerning the extra costs of caring for the child with disabilities, Table 2.2 shows the percentage of all Phase 2 parents in our study reporting a range of extra costs, compared to postal surveys of families with a child with severe disabilities from a range of minority ethnic groups (Chamba *et al.* 1999) and mainly White families (Beresford 1995). To cover these extra costs, over half the parents in our study reported that they themselves occasionally or often had to go without (55.6%) or borrow money (57.0%).

As Table 2.2 shows, many more parents in this study reported a whole range of extra costs associated with caring for their child compared to previous UK surveys (Beresford 1995; Chamba *et al.* 1999). These levels of extra costs may be due to low household incomes where such costs cannot easily be absorbed within household budgets. They may also be due to a lack of receipt of benefits and a lack of support from services. Indeed, similarities between our study and previous research (in terms of the extra costs of holidays, special equipment, child minding/babysitting, therapies for the

Table 2.2 Percentage of families reporting extra costs associated
with their child with disabilities: our study
versus Chamba *et al.* (1999) and Beresford (1995)

Item or service	Our study (all families) (%)	Chamba *et al.* (1999) (all ethnic groups) (%)	Beresford (1995) (majority White families) (%)
Clothing	89	79	63
Washing/laundry	87	74	78
Treats for disabled child	79	48	36
Heating	78	61	61
Bedding	77	65	57
Transport	75	52	53
Keeping disabled child occupied	73	55	48
Hospital visiting costs	71	54	50
Treats for other children	69	34	32
Food	65	49	28
Outings/leisure activities	61	45	39
Telephone bills	60	49	47
Replacing furniture/carpets	55	42	29
Home repairs	54	36	20
Toiletries/medical supplies	53	36	27
Holidays	48	45	49
Home adaptations	32	22	17
Moving house due to child	27	22	18
Medical consultation/treatment	23	12	6
Special equipment for child	21	25	16
Traditional healer	16	n/a	n/a
Child minding/babysitting	11	19	23
Therapies for child	10	15	11
Extra lessons for child	10	10	4
Help with housework	5	25	8
Other	3	5	0

child and help with housework) may be due to the impoverished lifestyles of families, where regular holidays are not undertaken and expectations of paid help for child minding and housework are absent. It is worth noting that in our study, at the suggestion of Phase 1 parents, we asked about the costs associated with traditional healers. Sixteen per cent of parents in Phase 2 mentioned that they were in contact with (and paying for) the services of a traditional healer.

Summary

For the 136 South Asian families with a child with severe disabilities in our study, a pattern of real disadvantage emerges, similar to the picture reported by Chamba *et al.* (1999). Household income is low, unemployment is high and housing is unsuitable for the needs of the family (particularly in terms of lack of space and safety issues). Transport is difficult for many families, with parents using a family car or taxis much more than public transport. Families in this study reported a wide range of extra costs associated with caring for the disabled child, with uptake of benefits appearing to be less than optimal. Although most families have two parents, a significant minority are single parent families, who experience even lower levels of household income. Families do not talk about the issues of housing, income, employment and benefits separately from issues of support from services. In the absence of supportive professionals and support from services, housing and economic problems appear to be worse.

Most main carers are mothers born outside the UK, who have spent many years in the UK and who care for the family full time. A substantial minority of families include more than one child with disabilities. Ethnic identity is stronger than national identity among these parents, less than half of whom speak, read or write English. Patterns of language use reflect specific ethnic groups and speech communities. Although the general picture in terms of ethnic identity and language use is similar to previous UK research (Chamba *et al.* 1999; Hatton *et al.* 1998), there are some important differences. These differences highlight the importance of attending in more detail to the specific characteristics of local communities. In any one area, the description of a community as 'South Asian', or even as 'Pakistani', 'Bangladeshi' or 'Indian', will not be enough to reliably identify religion, language and other important cultural aspects of that community.

Chapter Three

The Child

As in any family, the characteristics of a child with disabilities will have an important influence on the broader life of the family (Emerson 2003; Seltzer, Floyd and Hindes in press). This influence of a child with disabilities on the family has been shown across many countries and cultures (see Blacher 2001; Hatton 2002). This chapter describes some important aspects of the children with disabilities drawn from the Phase 2 interviews, with some richer descriptions of children from the Phase 1 interviews.

Basic characteristics of the child

Consistent with previous research (Emerson *et al.* 2001), most of the children with severe learning disabilities in Phase 2 were boys: 74 boys (55.6%); 59 girls (44.4%). Parents in Phase 1 and Phase 3 generally reported more worries about daughters than about sons, although parents reported a greater sense of lost expectations concerning their son with learning disabilities, particularly if he was the first-born child.

> The difficulties you have with daughters...she'd have had periods and we wouldn't be able to get her married. And I would have had so many problems. Someone could for example rape her. It could happen. She could become pregnant... I think of myself as lucky [for having a son with disabilities] and at that time I say 'God, thank you, whatever you do you do it for the best'.
>
> *Zareena*

If it's a boy then it's not as worrying if he wanders out. There is a concern about a daughter as when she is older the parents may have problems.

Hawra

It did seem difficult for everyone because in my husband's family he [child with disabilities] was the first child in that generation and my husband was an only child. It was very hard for the family to accept but it's God's will.

Zareena

He's [child with disabilities] my older son... He had to help me you know. And he had to stand shoulder by shoulder with me you know...had to be my successor I mean. So all these things... Because I am thinking I have lost my son you know.

Akram

The age range of the children was very wide (1 to 21 years; mean 11.5 years); including 22 children (16.2%) aged 1 to 5 years, 32 children (23.5%) aged 5 to 10 years, 47 children (34.6%) aged 11 to 15 years and 35 children (25.7%) aged 16 to 21 years. Parents in Phase 1 reported increasing practical and emotional problems as their child became older.

Girls of her age help their parents a bit. But poor Iman needs help and support from others. I need to take care of her in every way. When they [two daughters with disabilities] grow older it will become more difficult to look after them and take them out.

Azra

At first he's just a baby. It's later on in years that it [the disability] starts hitting you. When everybody else's kids are getting on with it and he's still back there.

Shahina

Especially as they [son and daughter with disabilities] are growing up the responsibilities increase and there is no help from anywhere. If I have to go somewhere in an emergency I can't leave the children with anyone. As I grow older and weaker things are going to get a lot more difficult. The support worker only helps me a little. I don't want to become ill for I need to take care of the children [two children with disabilities]. They need me.

Zora

He was very small before but now his legs are very long. I get very tired and I have asthma because of picking him up all the time and carrying him upstairs.

Faiza

Irfan is a poorly child. They [services] do help him a little, but I am thinking that he is growing day by day, his problems are increasing.

Samaya

Well he's reaching puberty so his body is going to be changing. He's still very young mentally and it's frightening me because he'll have all the feelings of a normal child and how am I going to cope with it?

Shahina

In terms of a diagnosis, many parents (44.8%) reported that their child had an unspecified learning disability, had special needs, or showed slow development; with several parents (9.0%) reporting unspecified brain damage. Commonly reported specific diagnoses were Down's syndrome (14.2%) and cerebral palsy (6.0%). A small number of parents (5.2%) reported that they did not know what their child's disability was. Different degrees of parental understanding of their child's disability could be seen from the descriptions given by Phase 1 parents.

She goes to a special school because she is different from other children. She does not understand anything… I feed her and change her clothes.

Halima

Well basically it's because of his disability and he's got chromosome 7 deletion. They haven't got a name for it. He's got a lot of developmental delay. He can't walk. He doesn't talk… Basically he can't do anything for himself.

Nasreen

The doctors said that you can't have high hopes for him [child with severe disabilities], because however much he develops, even if he begins walking, talking and everything he will never be normal. He will not really have the ability to study or talk because his brain has not developed properly.

Roshni

I don't understand why. It's just that she's ill and she's at the school. It's for her own benefit. She may not get better here at home and so she's at the school.

Hawra

Stable characteristics of the child

In the Phase 1 interviews, parents mentioned the importance of their child's personality. To explore this issue in the Phase 2 interviews, we asked parents about stable characteristics of their child with disabilities, using the 'Child Traits' section of the Caregiver Information Questionnaire (CIQ) (Kozloff *et al.* 1994). This asks parents how often over the past three to six months their child with disabilities had shown 15 different characteristics, such as being happy, sociable, sad and frustrated. We also scored these 15 characteristics into four scales: acting out/aggressive; sad/withdrawn; happy/affectionate; and co-operative. Children who were acting out/aggressive were also more likely to be sad/withdrawn. In contrast, happy/affectionate children were also more likely to be co-operative and less likely to be sad/withdrawn.

As Figure 3.1 shows, most parents reported their children to be happy, sociable and affectionate at least fairly often, although fewer parents reported their children to be co-operative and soothable this often. However, most parents also reported a wide range of acting out/aggressive traits in their child to occur at least fairly often, although sad and withdrawn traits were slightly less frequent. Overall, parents reported their child to be happy/affectionate most frequently, followed by acting out/aggressive, sad/withdrawn, and, least frequently, co-operative.

The only difference between ethnic groups was in acting out/aggressiveness, where Indian parents rated their children as less frequently acting out/aggressive than Pakistani and Bangladeshi parents. There were no differences in these child characteristics according to the age or gender of the child with disabilities.

Most parents in Phase 1 described the child as fitting well into the family, although others reported less sociable child traits that had a substantial impact on family life.

He [child with disabilities] fits in very easily. He's so happy and all the family are very happy with him... And if he hasn't been seen by someone he knows for one or two days the people start asking about him... If he

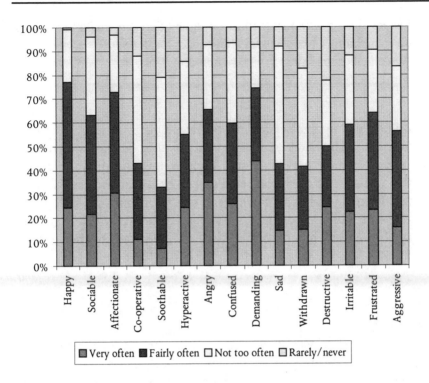

Figure 3.1 Child traits shown in the past three to six months

doesn't go out to the shops for one day, the next day the shop owners start asking my relatives… My children have fitted in very easily.

Zareena

He's just a lovable child…Oh you've got to see him. He's always always always got a smile on his face. He's got such a beautiful smile… Sometimes we get stopped by people: 'Oh, hasn't he got a lovely smile.' He's absolutely gorgeous he really is. I mean that's what gives me the most pleasure. He's such a nice boy. I mean if he's done something naughty he'll just give you a great big smile and he's just beautiful.

Nasreen

He gives me a lot of love and I really lap it up. He's a very happy child in himself. He's got a lot of love to give and he's just innocent when he's happy you know.

Shahina

I enjoy playing with him [child with disabilities] and would like him to do something as well. He will always play. He doesn't sit down quietly. When he becomes tired I will lay him down for a short while and play with him. It makes him happy.

Roshni

If we've got any problems in the family we can't discuss it in front of Sharukh... There are certain times you may be shouting at the children saying 'No, this is out of the way'. But in front of Sharukh you can't say that...because Sharukh will stand up and he'll start swearing at them. And we could be just sat down there. We are laughing and he'll get up and start hitting everybody... We really try to avoid discussing any family problems in front of Sharukh. We'd rather wait until he's gone to school.

Jabir

Child skills

The skills of the child with disabilities clearly have an important influence on the extent and nature of supports needed by families. Child skills were investigated in Phase 2 interviews using 24 questions from the Caregiver Information Questionnaire (CIQ) (Kozloff *et al.* 1994) asking about a wide range of child skills. We also scored these 24 specific child skills into four scales: self-care skills; communication skills; interest in activities; and social skills. Child skills were highly related to each other; children with skills in one area were highly likely also to have skills in other areas. Table 3.1 shows the individual child skills reported by parents in the Phase 2 interviews.

Table 3.1 shows huge diversity among the children in terms of child skills, although most children needed substantial help to display their skills. Most parents reported that their child could respond to familiar people and play by herself or himself without substantial help, and that their child fitted at least fairly well into the family. However, most parents also reported that the child needed lots of help with or could not engage in a wide range of self-care skills, household tasks, and any form of spoken communication.

There were no differences between ethnic groups in child skills. Older children were reported to have more self-care skills and communication skills, although interest in activities or social skills did not differ across child age groups. There were also no differences between boys and girls in any child skills. In the Phase 1 interviews, most parents seemed to adjust their expecta-

Table 3.1 Child skills reported by families

	Needs little help (%)	Needs some help (%)	Needs much help (%)	Needs lots of help (%)	Cannot do this (%)
Feeds self	24.6	29.1	11.9	9.7	24.6
Uses toilet	15.7	20.1	11.2	20.1	32.8
Washes hands and face	11.2	20.9	14.2	14.9	38.8
Puts one piece of clothing on/off	17.3	19.5	8.3	16.5	38.3
Dresses self	13.4	15.7	12.7	17.2	41.0
Responds to familiar people	34.1	34.1	21.2	6.8	3.8
Talks about goings on	18.7	20.1	8.2	16.4	36.6
Talks about being bothered or hurt	15.0	15.8	11.3	21.1	36.8
Talks about wants	16.5	19.5	10.5	20.3	33.1
Imitates holding/ stacking/throwing	21.6	27.6	18.7	11.9	20.1
Plays by self	20.3	36.8	14.3	15.0	13.5
Plays with others	8.2	27.6	21.6	20.9	21.6
Goes to bed at night	13.4	27.6	10.4	36.6	11.9
Puts things back in right place	10.4	12.7	17.9	28.4	30.6
Cleans table after eating	7.5	11.2	14.2	26.9	40.3
Does simple tasks	11.2	20.9	14.2	24.6	29.1
Makes simple food	7.6	8.3	8.3	10.6	65.2
Does activities outside home	6.0	30.8	15.0	26.3	21.8
Is skilful doing tasks	1.7 Very often	18.5 Fairly often	44.5 Not too often	35.3 Rarely or never	
Interested/involved in home activities	13.5 Very often	29.3 Fairly often	32.3 Not too often	24.8 Rarely or never	

Shows interest in family activities	14.2 Great interest	38.1 Some interest	17.9 Little interest	29.1 Very little interest	
Takes part in chores and games	3.8 Almost always	9.0 Frequently	19.5 Sometimes	66.9 Rarely or never	
Regular member of family	20.3 Fits in well	55.6 Fits in fairly well	18.0 Does not fit in well	6.0 Does not fit in at all	
Co-operates with requests	7.5 Always tries	26.9 Frequently tries	42.5 Sometimes tries	23.1 Rarely co-operates	

tions of their child's skills to the child's capabilities, so that the child's achievements and skills could be recognised and celebrated. However, a small number of parents focused on what the child could not do.

> I'm most happy at his memory (laughs) because when any of my brothers have a job to do I tell Bilal to remember the night before. Then I feel most happy when he gets up in the morning and says 'Mum, do you remember this job had to be done'... In fact we're all happy at his memory.
>
> *Zareena*

> ...he can do most of his work himself like changing his clothes, going to the toilet, eating, etc... He will also help the other children with their wheelchairs.
>
> *Duaa*

> He knows who everyone is. When he sees her [younger sister]...he goes wild. He's waving and screaming and a big smile on his face. And even now he'll do things. He'll copy things that she does.
>
> *Nasreen*

> Coping with him? He is unable to say anything. He has no speech, no movement [inaudible]. I feel disheartened.
>
> *Mariah*

However, parents in the Phase 1 interviews also described the constant care and attention that their child with disabilities required.

He's slow in what he does. He's got to be under supervision day and night basically. He can't be left alone like normal kids. He's got to be under supervision when he plays out. He's not aware of the danger on the roads and stuff like that.

Shahina

I change his clothes three to four times a day. He can't clean himself... We need two people to wash him, change his clothes and put on his nappy.

Zakiya

Child problem behaviours

Research has repeatedly shown that problem behaviours shown by a child with disabilities can have a negative impact on family life. In Phase 2 of our study, child problem behaviours were investigated using 12 problem behaviour questions from the Caregiver Information Questionnaire (CIQ) (Kozloff *et al.* 1994). Figure 3.2 shows, for each problem behaviour, whether the problem behaviour occurred and how much of a problem each behaviour was for parents.

All child behaviour problems were reported as occurring by most parents, with over 80 per cent of parents reporting problems associated with eating, toileting and bedtime routines, their child making a mess and throwing things, and their child yelling, screaming and throwing tantrums. All these problems except problems with eating habits were at least often a problem for parents.

There were no differences between ethnic groups in child problem behaviours. The only age-related difference in child problem behaviours was in yelling or screaming, with pre-school children mostly likely and teenage children least likely to show this behaviour. There were also no differences in child problem behaviours between boys and girls.

Parents in the Phase 1 interviews discussed how the presence of child problem behaviours could result in difficulties for the whole household, and a lack of support from extended family or friends.

There are times you know when he's not feeling too well. We are afraid to take him out. We can take him down in the car and he could be just showing two fingers at other people on the road...we're always scared somebody can lose his temper...so we've got to be very careful.

Jabir

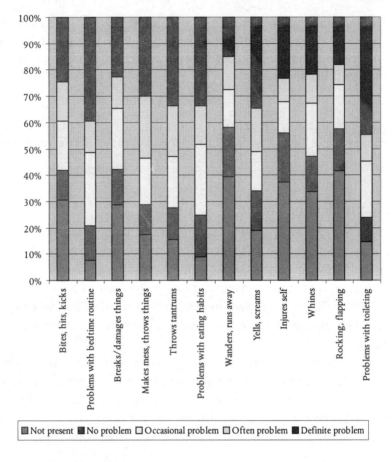

Figure 3.2 Child problem behaviours

If there is something in the house she [child with disabilities] just ruins it. She was with the other children and once or twice she has started a fire in the house.

Shaziza

You know you always have to keep with her [child with disabilities] and hold her hand wherever you go. You can't let her play outside by herself. She has to stay home where you always have to keep an eye on her. It's hard. When she gets mad she bangs on everything and pulls the curtains and sometimes she starts kicking the doors.

Sarah

I have problems now because Sayed's grown up… Even though he's got a lot of problems he is a cheeky boy and he'll do naughty things that he's not supposed to do… I have problems. Nobody wants to mind him because he's naughty.

Nasreen

She [child with disabilities] causes a lot of problems for the other children and we as parents have to take all the responsibility. We feel that she is a danger to our other children, because if a child is asleep she goes and hits them and therefore there is a danger of injury.

Halima

Child progress

As well as asking about behaviour problems, we felt it was important to ask about positive progress the child was making. The Caregiver Information Questionnaire (CIQ) (Kozloff *et al.* 1994) includes five questions about what progress the child has made in the past six months, and we asked these questions to parents in Phase 2. As with child skills, there was substantial diversity among the children in terms of child progress in the past six months. Almost half of parents felt that their child had learned and applied new skills in the past six months. Just over half of parents felt that these new skills were at least fairly important to them, and that their child was easier to live with compared to six months ago. However, around a third of parents felt that their child had learned no new skills in the past six months, and that the skills being taught to their child were not important. Finally, 16 per cent of parents felt that their child was harder to live with than six months ago.

There were no differences between ethnic groups in terms of individual aspects of child progress or overall child progress. There were also no differences in child progress according to the gender or age of the child. As with child skills, most parents in the Phase 1 interviews adjusted their expectations of child progress to the abilities of the child, so that progress could be recognised and celebrated.

…when he couldn't sit up, we had to sit him up and then I used to pray to God that you know just let him get to that stage where he sits himself up. If he wants to sit up he can sit up. If he wants to lie down he can lie down and thank God. I thank God that he's got to that stage – he can sit himself up.

Nasreen

When he [child with disabilities] says one or two words which are new then we feel very happy. 'Look he said, you know…and he's improving, you know.' So that is our happiness.

Akram

Some parents in the Phase 1 interviews also wanted information to help them to assist in their child's development at home, and they wanted education to continue throughout the child's adulthood.

Parents need an assessment of their child's skills and abilities to see what their child enjoys the most and what sort of skills the child has got. Then the parents can send them to places where they can improve the child's skills.

Jabir

As he is growing older he needs help with his homework and I should know how to help him with his education. The school should guide the parents on how to help their children and I have difficulty in helping him. He is very interested in reading and writing and asks me to help him and I help him in what I know, and what I do not know I cannot help him and the teachers should guide us on how to help our children in their work… We try to do whatever makes him happy. He is not much interested in toys, but he likes playing with educational toys, a small computer he has got. Sometimes I will help him to use it or his younger brother will help him.

Duaa

Disabled children are not complete vegetables and they should carry on improving their development [after 19]. Parents should be taught how to teach and help improve their child's development.

Roshni

Summary

As we would expect with any large group of children with disabilities drawn mainly from education services, the children with severe learning disabilities in our study were very diverse, with a slight majority of boys and a wide range of child ages. The largest single group of parents described their child as having unspecified learning disabilities. The most common specific conditions named by parents were Down's syndrome and cerebral palsy, although a small number of parents reported that they did not know what their child's disability was.

Children were diverse in their traits, skills and behaviours, although, as would be expected with a group of children with severe learning disabilities, most children needed substantial support across a range of self-care skills, household tasks and spoken communication skills. Most parents described their children as fairly happy, sociable and affectionate, and as fitting into the family relatively well. However, most parents also described their child as acting out or being aggressive at least fairly often, and over 80 per cent of parents reported the occurrence of problems associated with eating, toileting and bedtime routines, their child making a mess and throwing things, and their child yelling, screaming and throwing tantrums.

Around half of parents felt that their child had learned and applied important new skills in the past six months, and that their child was easier to live with than six months ago. Most parents seemed to adjust their expectations to the skills and progress possible for the child, enabling the family to recognise and celebrate the child's achievements.

Chapter Four

Information

Previous research with families from minority ethnic communities with a person with disabilities has emphasised the importance of information for families, particularly when English is not the first language of many family members (Mir *et al.* 2001). In the Phase 1 interviews parents also highlighted the importance of getting good information, in particular emphasising the importance of how they were told about the child's disability. To reflect this emphasis, we asked parents in the Phase 2 interviews how they were told about their child's disability, using the 47-question Index of Good Practice in Disclosure (Sloper and Turner 1993; Turner and Sloper 1992). This has previously been used mainly with White UK parents of children with severe physical disabilities. This chapter begins by describing parents' experiences of the disclosure process and its consequences, and goes on to discuss the general information needs of parents.

Disclosure

Previous UK research projects have identified being told about the child's disability as a crucial period for White parents with a child with a disability (Sloper and Turner 1993; Turner and Sloper 1992), although very little research has been conducted with South Asian parents (see Shah 1995, 1998). As many South Asian parents with a child with a disability are unlikely to use the English language, and professionals are unlikely to use any language other than English or to have access to a professional interpreter (see Chamba *et al.* 1999; Hatton *et al.* 1998), disclosure may be less than satisfactory for these parents. Parents in the Phase 1 interviews also talked at length about the disclosure process, as they viewed disclosure as having a fundamental impact on later parental understanding and acceptance of the child's disability, and on access to benefits and service supports.

The time of disclosure

As the children in our study were children with severe disabilities, disclosure of the child's disability generally occurred relatively early in the life of the child and most of the first diagnoses (64%) were definite. In the Phase 2 interviews, 3 per cent of parents had found out about the child's disability before the child's birth, 14 per cent had found out at the time of the birth and 83 per cent had found out some time after the birth; most of these parents found out by the time the child was 4 years old, although a small number of parents (3%) did not find out until their child was 11 or 12 years old.

Almost half the parents in the Phase 2 interviews (47%) had suspicions that their child had a disability before receiving a diagnosis. The most common reasons for parental suspicion were slow development, particularly in terms of walking or talking (49% of parents with suspicions), fits (11%), unusual behaviours (11%), child illnesses (11%), problems during pregnancy (5%) and the child's appearance (5%). Most parents (73%) discussed these suspicions with their GP, and most parents (81%) felt that their worries were taken seriously by the GP.

The disclosure process was most often conducted by a medical professional, usually a specialist consultant (71%), and occasionally by a GP (7%) or health visitor (4%). Perhaps of most concern was that some parents (9%) only learned about their child's disability at the special education service where the child had already been placed. One parent in a Phase 3 interview said of her 16-year-old child with disabilities:

> I want to know why. I still don't have the information.
>
> *Henna*

There were no differences between ethnic groups in these aspects of disclosure practice.

Language and information in disclosure

Parents in the Phase 2 interviews reported that most of the disclosures (67%) were carried out in English, although only 3 per cent of parents would have preferred to be told in English. Written information was given to only 33 per cent of parents. Almost all this written information was in English (88%), although few parents (8%) preferred written information in English. Of those parents who did not receive written information at the time of disclosure, over half (56%) would have wanted to receive some.

Around half of parents reported that they had received at least adequate information (58%), that they understood the information at least quite well (55%), that the language used was not too technical (48%), and that the information was at least quite easy to remember (62%). However, many parents reported receiving a poor quantity of information (19%), which they had found at least quite hard to understand (20%), at least quite technical (26%), and at least quite difficult to remember (16%). While most parents felt that the disclosing professional was a good communicator (62%), many felt that he/she was a poor communicator (16%).

There were few differences between ethnic groups. Bangladeshi parents reported greater understanding of the diagnosis given than Indian and Pakistani parents, and Indian parents were less likely to have been told in their preferred language than Bangladeshi and Pakistani parents.

Support during disclosure

Support at the time of disclosure was crucial for parents. For most of the parents in the Phase 2 interviews, both their partner (75%) and child (79%) were present at the time of disclosure. During the disclosure process, most parents felt that they had enough opportunity to ask questions (73%) and opportunity to contact the disclosing professional again after the time of disclosure (69%). Most parents found the disclosing professional was at least quite sympathetic (73%), understood parents' concerns at least quite well (66%), was at least quite approachable (64%) and was direct rather than evasive (76%). English-speaking parents reported that disclosure professionals were more direct.

However, support after the initial disclosure was lacking. Only a very small number of parents (5%) were offered help to tell the rest of the family, although 35 per cent of parents wanted this. Similarly, only 21 per cent of parents were put in contact with other families, although 47 per cent of parents wanted this also.

Overall, according to the criteria for good disclosure practice used in previous research (Sloper and Turner 1993; Turner and Sloper 1992), only 14.7 per cent of parents experienced good practice in disclosure.

The only difference between ethnic groups was that Indian parents were more likely to want help to tell the rest of the family than Pakistani or Bangladeshi parents.

Parental satisfaction with disclosure

In the Phase 2 interviews, just under half of parents were satisfied with the disclosure process (48%), with 21 per cent neutral and 31 per cent dissatisfied (there were no differences between ethnic groups in satisfaction). The Phase 1 interviews provided a very rich picture of why parents become satisfied or otherwise with the disclosure process.

Parents in the Phase 1 and Phase 3 interviews discussed how they would like to have been told about their child's disability. If they were told in the way they wished, their satisfaction with the disclosure process and their understanding of their child's disability increased. For parents, crucial aspects of a well-conducted disclosure process were:

- prompt disclosure (often in response to parental concerns)
- disclosure occurring with appropriate language support
- clear information about the child's disability and the practical implications of this for the family
- disclosure being handled in an emotionally supportive way
- disclosure being linked to support services being provided after disclosure
- disclosure being conducted with both parents present, where possible.

These aspects of good practice in the disclosure process were all essential; the absence of any one of them could result in parental upset, a lack of understanding and acceptance of the child's disability, and a lack of awareness and uptake of support services.

For many parents in the Phase 1 and Phase 3 interviews, disclosure occurred without appropriate language support, resulting in parental distress, limited parental understanding and a lack of uptake of supports. Some parents also described the distress of having to translate for their partners in the disclosure session.

> When she was 2 years old we were waiting that she will walk. We took her to the [English-speaking] doctor and he told us that she would walk. We were not happy [about the disclosure process] because she is dependent. She cannot feed herself and cannot walk or speak. She is dependent on us for everything. They [doctors] did not tell us [about the child's disability]. When she was 5 years old they started to pay us benefit.
>
> *Seema*

It might have helped if there was information in Asian... First nobody thought it was a big issue, even her father... It's very difficult to accept. Even now we have not accepted it.

Henna

Nobody explained to my husband in Punjabi. When I understood it then I had to tell my husband it all in Punjabi. It took a while for me to accept it... I didn't accept it until he got older. I think they didn't get the message across to me properly. They just said we'd have some difficulties, that's it. They didn't tell me about anything. No help from services at all.

Firdaus

Even if disclosure occurred in an appropriate language, a lack of empathy from disclosing professionals could have both short-term and long-term emotional consequences for parents.

I can remember that really well. And I can remember I was on my own [in the ward] and this one doctor came and told me. He said 'Your son has got a physical disability'. And he was a junior doctor and I'll never forget when he turned round and said to me, he said 'I'm afraid your son won't live beyond his teens'. And he just came out with it. The way he said it. I'll never forget it. You don't want someone to explain it like that. You want 'Come on Mrs X, do you want to sit down? I've got some news. I'm afraid it's bad but this is what it is. I'm afraid your son's got X condition. This is what it means'. There's a way of explaining it you know... It would have been easier if they'd made sure somebody was with me. I mean he's gonna be 6 next month but still it's very hard for me to accept.

Nasreen

Well I mean to them it was a very sort of casual relaxed sort of way, as if to say 'Yes he suffers from Down's syndrome. There's nothing to worry about. He's got no problems healthwise and here is your bundle of joy. And by the way here's a pile of papers. So if you want to go and find out how other people with Down's are developing and getting on, here's the file'... As far as I was concerned I rejected him. I denied he was my baby, because I was just expecting a perfectly healthy baby.

Shahina

They should give emotional support and information on the services available, instead of carers trying to endlessly search and find out about services over a long time.

Akram

Parents also reported that being told without their partner present was distressing, and could lead to differences in understanding and acceptance between parents.

He [husband] was at home looking after the little girl [at the time of disclosure]. My husband was very easy-going about it. It was sort of 'Oh well, he's here now', no feelings, no emotions. 'Well God sent him so we've got to accept him.' And I had so many years of anger packed up and regret of having this child, then basically it's been very very difficult.

Shahina

And he'd [husband] been away. And he said to me 'You weren't looking after yourself and that's why this has happened'. And he made me believe it and then my mum started saying it to me... I actually remember we went to the geneticist and I actually asked her to put it on paper that it wasn't my fault... It really had a bad effect on me and I went through that for about two years, three years even.

Nasreen

Vague or overly optimistic predictions of child progress from disclosing professionals were also seen as unhelpful by parents. They could hinder parental acceptance of their child's disability, leading to parents not applying for benefits or taking up support services.

He [hospital consultant] just said that she is behind with her age. He did not say how much or if there was anything to worry about...it's like we were kept in the dark for four years. We did not know anything. We treated her as a normal child. We did not feel any of her needs. Other children considered her as 'dumb'... He [husband] used to say that there is nothing wrong with her so there is no need to take her [to the doctor]... We did not understand anything about learning disability. Just that she is behind her age. I did not understand and my husband said there is not much wrong. So I told him that 'I think the doctor was saying about bringing a team of doctors at our home to examine all the family' but he [husband] said that there was nothing to worry about. Obviously I was very upset. I cried in the hospital and at home. Later our English health visitor arranged the special school. One day I went to the school and saw that all the children were disabled. I was very upset. I wept all the way home.

Henna

If I knew what to expect now, I don't think that I could have gone through with it [saving a sick premature baby]. The doctor could have given me an opportunity whether we wanted to carry on or not and told me more about that he's going to be severely handicapped and disabled. Instead of saying that the child might be all right.

Firdaus

What's going to happen? Nobody told me that. I've been really upset about that. I mean, is Umber going to be like that or is she going to get better? What is exactly wrong with her? I tried a lot of times. That's what I said. 'What's causing the troubles?' They just use the word 'She's mentally handicapped'... I like to be prepared... Everybody was upset and disappointed. No other members of the family have had a child like that or with disabilities... They didn't say anything to me about she's not going to talk and she's not going to be normal.

Arslan

The doctors have explained to us that he doesn't understand that others have pain...we stayed there for the whole day. The specialist checked Tahir and observed him do things and play... The doctors used an interpreter and told us that he has autism... He said his brain is undeveloped and he will be like this.

Zakiya

Parents found clear and detailed information as part of the disclosure process much more useful than vague or unrealistic predictions. A clear explanation of the child's disability could also help parents when telling other people about the child.

They should first call both parents and remove any cultural myths about learning disability. They should explain how the learning disability happened in the womb or after birth. They should explain all the medical reasons why and only the doctor can explain that. My friend thought it was a djinn and many Muslims believe that. The myths need to be removed. The doctors explained everything to me so I don't believe in all that.

Zareena

They [two English-speaking hospital consultants and an interpreter] told us what the problem was… That they've done some brain scans and Iman will have some problems mentally and physically. They told us quite clearly what the problem was and we were satisfied. We knew 'Yes, Iman did have a problem' and that problem was fully explained to us. After that speech and physiotherapists started to visit.

Azra

Parents also mentioned wanting to receive accurate information on the chances of their giving birth to a child with disabilities in the future, although this had to be conducted with cultural sensitivity.

When parents go through another pregnancy it is important for doctors to inform parents of the chances of that child also being disabled.

Zareena

A lot of people were not told that their child was severely disabled and may have gone on to have more children with disabilities. They should have been told about the chances of that happening… If an English person tells you 'Don't have more children', it comes out in the wrong way. It is better to be informed by an Asian person as there is a greater cultural, religious understanding. Carers would also be less suspicious of the loyalties of the Asian professional.

Henna

Parents were satisfied with the disclosure process when it contained all the aspects described above: clear information relayed in the appropriate language to both parents, in an emotionally supportive manner, resulting in service supports to the family.

The doctor told us that his brain has been damaged and whatever help you need we will provide for you. Many different types of people would come. First of all they gave us the washing machine and then the social worker would come to our house. The doctor told us at four months that he [child with disabilities] will not get better. He told us in English and there was also an Asian doctor there who would tell us. We were told in the proper way. The doctor just said that it was in your destiny.

Faiza

We went there and they told us everything properly... We were told that this is how it will end and this is their condition and we have not got a treatment to cure them [three children with disabilities]. Also we have to look after them as time goes by... We did ask them questions... He told us everything in detail... He told us in our language... He did not use difficult language. As a doctor he explained to us fully, the way he should have he did.

Farida

It was explained that with this child we'll have to train him this way... I was told about his feeding and his play. I was given a lot of information about his care that he needs more support and attention...he is a special child. I believe that nobody could have informed me better than she [health visitor] did...she told me very calmly and explained the whole future too...she helped me a lot to accept my child was disabled.

Zareena

He [hospital consultant] arranged the physio, dietician and all these things for him [child with disabilities]. He helped a lot and would tell me that I can get this type of help or that help. He also said that I could have a health visitor and arranged the disability allowance that I receive... I can get help with transport and help with an interpreter... The hospital quickly arranged help for [name of child], like the exercise class. He even started school at a very young age. I was also shown that other people have disabled children too, not just me.

Roshni

The doctor told me about the different categories of disability and 'We don't know which level your son is going to be yet, but some are very severe and some are less'. And he was saying he's got cerebral palsy. He broke it gently to me. He put his hand on my knee and he said to me you know 'I know it's going to be hard for you. You're young and you didn't deserve this, but no matter how hard I say it or how easy, there is no easy way to tell you about it'. He was very nice to me the way he said it... And afterwards I broke down and he said 'Take her in another room and comfort her and settle her down a bit' [husband was present]. And then he said that 'I'll see you in a couple of weeks'. And then he involved the social worker.

Amani

They introduced us to some families who have Down's syndrome babies so as to give us an idea of how to deal with this and what sort of attention Faizal would need. So I found out the next day really... They told us in detail what kind of children they are, the reason they're born this way and what help they would need. They could not tell us...what progress he would make. We would have to learn with time... We had never even heard or seen a case like that in our family.

Duaa

General information needs

Several UK studies suggest that parents across all ethnic groups lack information concerning the child's disability and the availability of benefits and service supports (Baxter *et al.* 1990; Beresford 1995; Chamba *et al.* 1999). Some researchers have suggested that due to limited use of English, a lack of information in languages other than English and poor interpreting support, parents in some minority ethnic communities may report a greater need for information (Baxter *et al.* 1990; Chamba *et al.* 1999; Mir 2001). In our study, parents' varied experiences of disclosure might also suggest that the need for information would be high among the families in this study.

In the Phase 2 interviews, parents were asked whether they had enough information about the child's disability, services for the child and supports for them as parents. Table 4.1 presents information for each ethnic group, with comparison information from the Chamba *et al.* (1999) postal survey. As Table 4.1 shows, fewer parents in our study reported having enough information in all areas than the parents in the Chamba *et al.* (1999) study. Parents across ethnic groups in our study reported similar levels of information about their child's disability. However, Bangladeshi parents were more likely than Indian and Pakistani parents to report that they had enough information about services for the child and supports for them as parents. Unlike in the Chamba *et al.* (1999) study, parents with English language fluency were more likely to have their information needs met. In particular, parents were more likely to report having enough information about services for the child if they could speak, read and write English.

Table 4.1 Percentage of parents having enough information and how they would like to obtain information: Phase 2 parents versus Chamba *et al.* (1999)

	Our study			Chamba *et al.* (1999)		
	Indian (%)	Pakistani (%)	Bangladeshi (%)	Indian (%)	Pakistani (%)	Bangladeshi (%)
Enough information about…						
Child's disability	61	52	53	71	66	82
Services for child	13	23	60	41	36	61
Support for parents	13	17	60	38	31	57
Would like more information through…						
A named worker	96	94	64	42	52	51
Professionals	91	90	36	43	32	34
Parent support group	64	59	0	29	19	13
Advice centre	46	61	54	41	23	33
Telephone helpline in English	59	31	23	22	14	10
Telephone helpline in other language	36	57	62	16	19	21
Written information in relevant language	50	55	46	48	48	31
Videos on child's disability	77	66	39	34	32	36
Videos on services	82	64	31	34	28	33
Local Asian media	55	65	46	n/a	n/a	n/a

We also asked parents in the Phase 2 interviews about special educational needs (SEN) statements, which all children with severe learning disabilities should have. Only just over half of Phase 2 parents (54%) reported that their child had a statement of SEN, a further 18 per cent reported that their child did not have a statement of SEN, and 28 per cent reported that they did not know whether their child had a statement of SEN or not. In addition, only just over half of parents (53%) reported understanding the statementing process. When parents did know that their child had a statement of SEN, almost all parents (95% of those receiving a statement of SEN) at least quite agreed with its content.

Table 4.1 also gives information about how parents would like to receive more information, compared to results from Chamba *et al.* (1999). Overall, parents in this study were more likely to report wanting information from a wide of range of sources compared to the families in Chamba *et al.* (1999), with the vast majority of parents wanting to receive information from a keyworker or other professional. All options, with the exception of a telephone helpline in English, were endorsed by more than half the parents. There were, however, some striking differences in preferences for information across ethnic groups. Bangladeshi parents were much less likely than Indian and Pakistani parents to report wanting to receive more information via a keyworker, professional, parent support group, telephone helpline in English or a video about services. This may be because more Bangladeshi parents report they already have enough information, although the practical implication is still that information will need to be tailored to the preferences of specific communities.

Most parents in the Phase 1 and Phase 3 interviews also reported that they desperately needed more information about services, as this information was crucial for gaining access to services. As with parents in the Phase 2 interviews, the preference was to receive information in the relevant language from a professional with an ongoing relationship with the family, although parents emphasised that a range of sources of information would be needed to meet individual family preferences.

> I would like someone Asian to come to my house and explain in my own language. I can also ask questions in my own language as to what I should do.
>
> *Hawra*

We would like information through a key professional, as you can also ask other related questions and clarify things. A video would give you the information but not clarify things. Information in the Pushto language would be best.

Akram

Someone female should tell me about services at home as it helps a lot. If someone writes it is more of a burden to have it read and write back. With a video I will listen to it alone and it will take too much time. I want someone to tell me in my own language as it will be easier for us to understand each other. It will enable me to ask anything there and then and understand fully.

Zora

The Urdu videos would be better [than Urdu leaflets] as it would benefit the many parents who cannot read. This will also satisfy the parents more as you can see the services on screen. There should also be an information number in Urdu and other different languages.

Zareena

In the absence of information from professionals, information was also sometimes gained from family or friends, although this was rare.

There were quite a lot of things that they could have explained to me. Like what my rights were. Like sending this child to a special school and all that which I don't know. I never knew there were special schools in this country, see? And I'm saying if when I found out that he could have a problem; if somebody from the social services, or from the health department, the health visitor or anybody would have got involved with us they might have given us some guidance about his future. And we might have sent him to a special school right from the first day when he went to school, instead of sending him to a mainstream school. At that time what I wanted was information.

Jabir

I think when you bring a small baby home and he's disabled...should be somebody there that has experienced talking to people and has met people. There's Asian people that have got nobody who can talk Asian or Punjabi about the facilities. Even my social worker didn't know what facilities were available for people with severe learning disabilities. There was nothing open on hand at the hospital or the social workers hadn't got time. There was nothing that said that there was any respite or anything at all.

Firdaus

The social worker has shown me that there are supports available in this country and she went everywhere with me... I get help with everything.

Huda

The social worker and our doctor they were going just to tell us that for him you can apply for...these are the things you know. And there were some things which we didn't understand and we didn't know about it and no one told us. But we heard it from friends that, well, you should do this and you should do that. My wife used to wash nappies you know and her fingers were infected.

Akram

When parents did receive information on an ongoing basis, this could be crucial for gaining access to benefits and services.

As he was the first child [with disabilities] we did not know what we needed. In the beginning the social worker guided us for a year and by then we got to know a lot. After that the school used to send us letters asking us if we were getting all the benefits or not. They told us what benefits we were entitled to... We received lots of information from the school.

Duaa

Summary

As the children had severe learning disabilities the majority of diagnoses occurred either around the time of the child's birth or before the age of 4 years. Almost half of parents had suspicions about their child's disability before a formal diagnosis had been made, with most parents expressing their concerns to their GP.

Most parents were told about their child's disability by a specialist medical professional, although some parents were told about their child's disability from special education professionals after their child had been placed there. Two-thirds of disclosures were in English, despite this being the preferred language of very few parents. Written information was provided to only one-third of parents, and was also mostly in English. Generally, about half of parents reported that they had understood what was said to them at the time of the disclosure, and most parents reported receiving good support from their partners (when present) and the disclosing professional. Support for parents after they were told about their child's disability, however, in terms of helping to tell extended families or putting parents in contact with other parents, was lacking.

For parents in the Phase 1 interviews, crucial factors increasing their satisfaction with the disclosure process and their understanding of their child's disability were: prompt disclosure (often in response to parental concerns); disclosure occurring with appropriate language support; clear information about the child's disability and the practical implications of this for the family; disclosure being handled in an emotionally supportive way; disclosure being linked to the support services; and disclosure being conducted with both parents present, where possible. These aspects of good practice in the disclosure process were all essential; the absence of any one of them could result in parental upset, a lack of understanding and acceptance of the child's disability, and a lack of awareness and uptake of support services.

Most parents in the Phase 2 interviews reported having enough information about the child's disability, although fewer parents reported having enough information about services for the child and for themselves as parents. Parents reported preferring to receive information in the appropriate language during face-to-face contact with a professional with whom they had an ongoing relationship. Parents were more likely to report having enough information if they could speak, read or write English.

Chapter Five

Informal Support

Families with a child with disabilities can receive support from a wide range of sources. This chapter focuses on the informal support received by families; the support given by people's relatives, friends, neighbours and other organisations outside the service system such as religious organisations (Quinton 2004). When talking about support, it is important to be clear about what we mean (see Quinton, 2004, for a discussion of the meaning of the word support). The meaning of support includes:

- the source of support (for example family, friends, religious organisations, different professionals and services)

- the extent of support offered (for example how many people or organisations offer support, how frequently and for how long?)

- the type of support offered (for example emotional support or comfort, advice, information, practical help, financial help)

- how support is experienced by the person on the receiving end. (Although people or organisations may be well-intentioned in offering support, parents may feel this support to be irrelevant or actively unhelpful.)

When asking parents about support, we were careful to make sure that we paid attention to all these aspects of support, to gain a rich picture of how families experienced and used the supports available to them. Parents in Phases 1 and 3 of our study were asked extensively about informal supports from both family members within the household and from extended family and friends outside the household. Parents in the Phase 2 interviews were asked about the availability and helpfulness of nine different sources of informal support over the past three to six months, using the Family Support Scale (Dunst, Trivette and Deal 1988). Other questions about informal support from the Chamba *et al.* (1999) postal survey were also asked of parents in the Phase 2 interviews.

Support within the household

Parents in the Phase 2 interviews were asked several questions concerning the support received from other people within the household, including help from the spouse or partner and help from other children.

Sixteen parents (11.8%) were lone parents and thus received no practical or emotional support from a spouse or partner in the household. Within two-parent families, most parents reported receiving substantial practical and emotional support from partners. This is similar to other UK studies of families with a child with severe disabilities across a range of ethnic groups (Beresford 1995; Chamba *et al.* 1999). Among two-parent families, 35.6 per cent of parents reported sharing practical help equally between parents, 16.5 per cent reported their partner helping a lot, 33.9 per cent a little and 13.9 per cent reported receiving no practical help from their partner. Higher levels of emotional support were reported, with 56.5 per cent of parents reporting equal emotional support between parents, 13.0 per cent receiving a lot of emotional support from their partner, 19.1 per cent receiving little support and 11.3 per cent receiving no emotional support from their partner. Partners were the most helpful source of informal support rated by parents. Unlike the parents in the Chamba *et al.* (1999) postal survey, there were no differences between ethnic groups in the amount of support received from partners.

Many parents also reported other children in the household helping with the care of the child with disabilities. Of all families, 35.1 per cent reported another child helping a lot and 30.5 per cent reported another child helping a little with the care of the disabled child. A quarter of parents (25.2%) said their other children were too young to help, 4.6 per cent said their other children did not help and 4.6 per cent had no other children. When other children in the household helped, they were generally rated as helpful by parents.

Most parents in the Phase 1 interviews reported receiving most of their informal support from within the household, in terms of practical and emotional support from partners and practical help from other children. Partners' involvement in practical support also revealed the importance for parents of intimate care tasks being carried out by a parent of the same gender as the child where possible. Parents also reported that they turned to their other children for support only in desperation, although parents were concerned about the impact of this support on their other children (Shah and Hatton 1999).

> He [husband] cares for them more than me, but because they are girls I cannot ask him to change their nappies…but he will take them upstairs and bring them down in the morning… He really cares for them. The little one doesn't sleep without her dad. She loves her dad a lot.
>
> *Azra*

> It causes difficulties. I'm talking about the culture. Men taking men's problems, but a man taking woman's, this sort of thing I'm not keen on it. I'm not very happy with that. I look at it that it's not right.
>
> *Arslan*

> To tell you the truth I think I put a lot of pressure on my daughter [without disabilities]…because if Sayed's not well she'll end up making something for the others to eat… Even our 9-year-old, our son… I'll say well you hoover up… She'll show me her schoolwork diary and she'll say 'I've got such and such an amount of homework to do Mummy. If I don't do it I'm gonna get demerit at school. It's up to you. If you want me to help you I'll help you, but if you want me to do my homework I'll do my homework'. I feel sorry for her… If she chooses to help me she'll get into trouble from the teachers. If she does the homework and she doesn't help me then I get annoyed because she's not helping me.
>
> *Nasreen*

> My other [7-year-old daughter] helps me a lot looking after Iman. When I am cooking she will feed Iman, or when I am cleaning upstairs she will look after Iman. They play together. At bedtime she will play games or music and then sleep with her. Afterwards I put her on a separate bed…she helps me more than her age.
>
> *Azra*

> My [14-year-old] daughter is having to be a carer which is not fair on her. So I really really don't have anyone to turn to. You get people visiting, you go to meetings but there's really nothing really done. Deep down I feel as if I've given up the fight. I feel like telling everybody I've not got time for all this shit.
>
> *Shahina*

Other children in the household were reported by parents in the Phase 1 interviews to show consideration and love to the child with severe disabilities, although feelings of jealousy also sometimes arose.

> I believe these children benefit through the development of feelings of softness towards the child with disabilities. For example, my son is more considerate towards his three learning disabled brothers. He is also more caring towards other children with disabilities.
>
> *Zareena*

> He is treated as normal, but the whole family loves him more than our other boys... They [child's siblings] love him a lot. They do not let him feel any different and when they go away they kiss him a lot. My eldest son goes to university and phones Faizal daily. They are not satisfied until they have talked to each other... Both brothers love him a lot.
>
> *Duaa*

> They [child's siblings] are very good to him. Everyone finds him adorable. They all talk to him and he [child with disabilities] will move his eyes towards the sound, but he cannot talk. They all care about him a lot and ask 'Mum, has he gone to school? What time will he be back?'
>
> *Faiza*

> And the boys, the children are good to Amir as well. They're always passing things, bringing food. But sometimes they get annoyed the children do, because they'll say that 'Oh, we can't do this or we can't do that because you've got a hospital appointment today. You've got to take him [child]'... They say that 'We've got to stop at home with Amir, and why is it all the time it's Amir?' You know like children feel it don't they. That parents are giving so much time to them when they could give it to us sometime.
>
> *Firdaus*

> Every now and again the kids get jealous sometimes... I think the little one she sometimes gets a bit jealous that, oh you know, 'Why is mum always holding Sayed?'... Sometimes she resents him but they're all very good with him, especially the little one. If she's got anything to eat or drink, anything, it doesn't matter what it is, it'll go to Sayed first.
>
> *Nasreen*

A lack of support from the partner was reported by parents as making life practically difficult and was a source of emotional distress for parents in the Phase 1 interviews. As discussed in Chapter 4, parental understanding and acceptance of the child's disability was crucially influenced by the disclosure process. This parental understanding and acceptance could also have an impact on the amount of support offered by the partner, and on parental contact with services.

> My husband wasn't very happy about sending Bilal to a disability nursery. My husband is very weak at heart. I controlled myself... In my husband's family there were no other children, just Bilal. So my husband did not want to accept that 'My child compared to other children is less able'. He'd say 'No, he's weak yet...when he grows older he'll be completely well'... When Bilal's disability allowance was due to start my husband wouldn't claim it.
>
> *Zareena*

> Me and my husband have not spoken about this. He has not felt it, neither did he ask me about it... I think until today he has never thought about it particularly... If I was to say that I am happy with my husband or I have his support or family support, these are things I do not have. My personal life is not good and my life with my children [three disabled children] is also hard.
>
> *Farida*

> He [husband] also doesn't like going to his [disabled child's] appointments and so I arrange transport and an interpreter...the problem is he will not go to the appointments with me.
>
> *Roshni*

> They [doctors] said that because of the long history of marriage within the family it is the reason for Nadia's illness to become more complicated and taken this form. Obviously no one wanted to hear this. When the doctors used to ask us if there was anyone in the family with this illness I wanted to say yes [brother-in-law] but my husband would tell me off... I was her mother. I wanted them [doctors] to know... Even now if I say it my husband gets angry.
>
> *Henna*

We did not blame each other for it as some couples may, as the doctors explained to us that nobody is to blame for this… Because of the help we had at the beginning [meeting other parents and having a keyworker] we did not have too much difficulty.

Duaa

For most parents, decision-making within the family was shared by both parents (where two parents were present), with mothers as the main carers slightly more likely to initiate and be involved in major decisions about the child with disabilities (92.3% of mothers and 83.1% of fathers in Phase 2). The child with disabilities was less likely to be involved in decision-making (34.3% of children involved at least occasionally), as were other children in the household (23.5% involved), relatives outside the household (9.3%) and professionals (10.1%).

Many of the parents in Phase 1 compared their family life to that of a 'normal' family with a child without disabilities. Many parents strove to achieve this sense of 'normality'. This was made easier by a combination of child characteristics and positive attitudes towards the child from family and friends. This 'normality' was usually described in terms of participating in an active social life as a family.

They've been very good with him, my sisters, my mum… They, everybody in my family, just acts like he's a normal child…my husband's the same.

Amani

If we're going out I use the pushchair. We're just a normal family. We visit family, they visit us. We go to Blackpool, Chester Zoo and the parks. My nieces also take him out.

Zareena

There are certain things that we can do with Sayed and there's certain things that we can't. It's like if I want to go shopping I can't go shopping. I can't take Sayed he's too big… I can't get him in the shopping trolley, I can't take him shopping, he's too big for his pram. I don't have the wheelchair at home…they won't give it to me because they say they need it in school. So Sayed is not allowed to go shopping. He can't go because there's no way that I can get him there…there's no other way [to obtain a wheelchair]… And the social services have done nothing at all.

Nasreen

Support outside the household

In contrast to the relatively high levels of support received within the house-hold, relatively low levels of support were reported from extended family, friends and other sources of informal support.

Support from extended families

Over two-thirds of parents in the Phase 2 interviews reported no help from extended family networks (67.7%), with 21.3 per cent reporting a little help and only 11.0 per cent reporting a lot of help from extended families. These are lower levels of support than those reported by parents from minority ethnic communities in the Chamba *et al.* (1999) postal survey. This was partly due to a lack of available support: over one-third of families in the Phase 2 interviews reported that neither their nor their partner's extended family lived nearby (37.4%). Indeed, parents most commonly identified extended families not living nearby as the major reason why extended families did not help (37.5%).

Where extended families did offer support, the nature of that support could be very diverse, including emotional support (27.2%), help looking after the disabled child (24.3%) and other children (22.8%), gifts or loans to the family (18.4%), help around the house (17.6%), help for the family to attend appointments (13.2%), help with transport (12.5%) and help with interpreting (8.1%). When this support was received it was generally much appreciated by the parents in the Phase 1 interviews. This view was endorsed by parents in the Phase 2 interviews. Although support from the parents' parents was often not available, when received their support was seen as more helpful than the more frequently available support from other relatives.

> My sister-in-law, I ask her advice first about what I should do because she has more knowledge than I do…she phones the agencies or the school to ask what we have to do. Then the school will respond by advising my sister and then she will explain to me. She finds out everything for me. My husband is like me, for that reason my sister will do everything.
>
> *Zareena*

> It [extended family support] makes it easier if you have problems. I can understand if we had no relatives or friends here then it would be very difficult just relying on outside help.
>
> *Akhmal*

My husband, my sister, Faizal's grandparents. Everyone helped us a lot. Even the doctors said he was lucky to have such a big family... He will learn from listening to others talk and seeing other children do things and mimicking them. We do not feel that our life is restricted because of him at this time... Even if we have to go somewhere we leave him with his aunt.

Duaa

A variety of reasons apart from unavailability were also given for the lack of support from extended families. Practical problems such as extended family members being too busy to help were cited (27.2%), although parents also reported extended family members not being interested in the child (16.9%) and not knowing help was needed (12.5%). However, many parents had not asked extended family members for support. This was for a variety of reasons: because parents felt the child was their responsibility (33.1%); because parents felt extended family members were too busy (21.3%); because extended family members couldn't cope with the disabled child (20.6%); or because extended family members didn't understand (18.4%). These responses suggest that informal support, even where available, is not automatically offered to families with a child with disabilities. Furthermore, the extent to which parents seek support from extended families is influenced by parental perceptions of extended family attitudes towards the child, and parental perceptions of their own roles and responsibilities regarding the disabled child.

Parents in the Phase 1 interviews reinforced this complexity of parental views concerning the nature and helpfulness (or otherwise) of extended family support. In particular, extended family members were less likely to be contacted and asked for support if they were seen as not understanding the needs of the child. If parents themselves were finding it difficult to accept the child's disability, support from the extended family was also less likely to be sought.

The other problem is family. Family can help in bad times but I have not got anyone here. All of my husband's family is here, but no one supports me. They do not talk to us.

Farida

I would say we're very worried about his [child with disabilities] school holidays. I was thinking that we will let him go to the relatives...but it's better if he's looked after by social services, because if he's got any problems when he's with relatives they won't know what to do.

Jabir

They [extended family] just come sometimes and stay for an hour and talk and then go away. They never give me any practical help. They just talk.

Zora

It doesn't matter how much my family is there for me, or you know, or friends are there. They don't understand... If they'll come to the house they'll say 'Oh well, Sayed's not well. Oh right'. As soon as they walk out of that door the problem's gone away.

Nasreen

They [extended family] treat Nadia all right, but no one gives her any status. It is as if she was just there, that's all... Children treat her better than adults. They have quickly learned that Nadia's needs are different. They treat her with understanding and sympathy... It is as if he [husband] has forgotten that Nadia is a part of the family. Sometimes I get angry at him that Nadia needs some attention.

Henna

My family are very good with him [child with disabilities], thank you to God. They don't think of him as a disabled child...everyone in the family loves him very much.

Roshni

When I used to see my relatives they used to sort of always find the funny side of him [child with disabilities] and I used to get offended by that. He'd have behaviour problems and because he was only there for that hour or two they would always look at the funny side of it but for the rest of the fortnight it was for me to make him feel that that's not appropriate... So basically in the end I just started seeing less and less of family really.

Shahina

It is pointless telling them [extended family] anything because straightaway they will say 'He'll get better'... I don't really get any support from family, right. And I don't ask for it any more. Even if I'm really desperate I'll kill myself. I'll kill myself and do it myself. I had so many friends and family [in Pakistan]. I do have family here but no one has the time to sit with anyone and talk... My in-laws are here, but everyone is busy with their own lives.

Arslan

We did not want to tell the family. But whenever they came he would not take any notice and just play. Then they found out there was something different about him. Then we had to force ourselves to tell them that he cannot speak and about the doctor's report... God gave us normal children before him so I did not want to tell anyone that he was not normal [begins to cry].

Zakiya

Parents in the Phase 1 interviews also reported that extended family members held a range of views concerning the causes of the child's disabilities and the possibility of 'cure'. Parents usually found such views unhelpful, although if parents had a good understanding of their child's disability, gained through effective disclosure, they could provide their families with more helpful interpretations of the child's disability.

People kept on saying take him down to the healers, do this, do that...like in Pakistan or India a lot of people say 'Oh he's got the devils in him. He's got this and he's got that see'. But I was shown all these scans see. This is this and this is this... I know that I've got medical evidence there. I've got the scans. I've been shown scans of a normal person and I've been shown his scans and I can see the differences. I've been told 'Well, this part of the brain is not normal'. It's very, very underdeveloped and what can spiritual healers or anybody do about that...there's nothing which any spiritual healer or a homeopathic doctor or any herbal doctor can do... So I just said 'I've been shown. I've been given proof of that. This child's brain is underdeveloped'.

Jabir

A lot of people felt sorry for me because I had a disabled child. I don't think anybody thought 'Oh you know, it's not me whose suffering it's my son'... My mum turned round and said to me 'Don't mix Sayed's clothes with theirs [other children] because he's different... Don't put the baby near him [child with disabilities]'. I said, 'Well, she's his sister'... Asian people don't understand... I kind of like put my mum straight... She kind of like understands now but it took six years.

Nasreen

Support from friends

Few families in the Phase 1 interviews reported receiving support from friends. As with family support, such support could be practical or emotional, although parents in the Phase 2 interviews rated support from friends as verging on the unhelpful. These ratings were endorsed by some parents in the Phase 1 interviews, who felt uncomfortable talking about their child with disabilities to their friends.

> My friend lives across the road. She comes every other day. If I'm having difficulties or I'm ill then she will come and make the chapattis and will do the jobs that my daughters can't do.
>
> *Hawra*

> As time goes by the good days are becoming very scarce. I cry a lot and sometimes talking to my friends takes my mind off these things.
>
> *Zora*

> To be quite honest with you I don't discuss a lot of personal things with my friends... They used to come... go for a walk and we'll go for a brew and we'll have a chat and they were good as well but I was more... it was within the family.
>
> *Amani*

In addition, some parents in the Phase 1 interviews felt that their friends did not understand about the child's disability, and so were not seen to be supportive.

> It was like a punishment or like what have I done to deserve this? They [family and friends] weren't helpful or supportive. They didn't understand.
>
> *Firdaus*

For some Phase 1 parents, other parents with a child with disabilities, usually met through the school, became invaluable sources of support, as they were seen as the only people who could truly understand what parents were experiencing.

> When I go to the school they [other parents] tell me about their child and I tell them about my child. This helps by making my heart feel at peace, after seeing each other and meeting each other as friends.
>
> *Faiza*

I mean maybe you sympathise, but nobody can understand my problem unless they've been down that road themselves... Last Christmas there was a concert at school and Sayed was in the play as well. I went to watch and I got chatting to one of the mums there, an English lady. And we got chatting about our problems and for the first time, for the first time since I've had Sayed, I really felt she really understood what I was talking about. Why? Because she had a child in the same position. And she said to me as well she said 'Yes, you know it's nice talking to another mum of a child with a disability because you understand where I'm coming from, you understand why I'm saying this'. It was really nice talking to her. I mean the other day she phoned me up and we were on the phone for two hours, but it's because we can relate to each other.

Nasreen

Support from local communities

Some parents in the Phase 1 interviews reported negative attitudes, stigma and a consequent lack of support from people in local communities.

I find that people are like afraid that they don't pick him up. They don't cuddle him, they don't kiss him. They talk to my other children, play with them, but not him. To me it seems like they'll come in and they'll sit on the other side as though he's got a disease or something that you can catch. Us Asian people have not got the message across. I think that there's something wrong somewhere.

Firdaus

In English they say disability, but in our language they say mental... The English say the child is special, but if we tell people outside that she is disabled they say she is mental. No one believes that she is any different. Instead they tell me that I am mad, that she will be cured.

Henna

Religious supports

Many of the Phase 1 parents reported that their religious faith was important for them in terms of understanding and accepting their child and helping them to cope.

Yes I do [have concerns for the future], but I also think and satisfy myself that what time has passed for me up till now and God has made it pass by so easily. Then maybe when that time comes, I am worrying at this time, but maybe at that time I won't be as worried. How do I know I may also manage that time so easily, that it would not even affect me. That I'll say 'Oh, I was stupid that I used to think about it for so long that this may happen or that may happen'. I remain dependent on God a lot [laughs].

Zareena

We have to accept the burden and Allah helps you to cope.

Ayesha

I wanted to go there [Pakistan] you know. And go to the worship places there and pray there in my own way to God… And I went everywhere with him… I was thinking in my mind that if I do a lot for him at least I know that I've done something. It helped me a lot.

Amani

However, families with a child with severe learning disabilities appeared not to seek or receive practical or emotional support from religious organisations. Parents were sometimes encouraged by other family members to take their child with disabilities to a traditional or religious healer. However, in the previous three months only a small number of Phase 2 parents reported going to a Hakim, Vaid or other traditional healer (1.5%) or a religious healer (1.5%). Consultation with a religious healer did not stop parents seeking and receiving other support services.

As Muslims we believe in Allah and my father advised me to take her [child with disabilities] to the Molvi [religious healer]… He [Molvi] said 'You should have come before because it's too late… It might have worked'.

Arslan

Disabled children should be able to go in and out of mosques and there should also be a community centre there to meet needs such as feeding, wheeling around and toileting. It should be there for a couple of hours to give carers a break.

Firdaus

Relatively few parents in the Phase 2 interviews reported at least sometimes receiving help from a local religious organisation or religious healer (10.3%), although religious organisations were more often viewed as unhelpful (44.1%) or not available for support purposes (45.6%). None of the parents in the Phase 2 interviews reported actively seeking practical or emotional support from local religious organisations.

> And our mosques are not doing anything for the disabled children. Where's all the money and funding going into? They're getting the funding from the community and I think they could have helped us... It's all right them doing a one-day food for old people...this [disability] is a need just as any other need. Like they should pay people to come out – not actually give us money in hand – but people to come out and help us, giving us a hand. Are you with me?
>
> *Firdaus*

Summary

By far the most common sources of informal support for families in our study were the partner or other children within the household, and this support was seen as helpful by most parents. Many parents reported receiving informal support from their own and their partner's relatives and friends and religious organisations, although the helpfulness of this support varied. The general picture is one of isolation for South Asian families with a child with severe disabilities.

Chapter Six

Formal Support

As earlier chapters have shown, South Asian families with a child with severe learning disabilities experience substantial disadvantages. Many families are living in housing which is unsuitable and unsafe for the needs of the child and do have not enough income to meet the extra costs of caring for the child with disabilities. Most of the children with disabilities need intensive support, and many families are single parent families or are caring for more than one child with disabilities. Although many parents receive valuable practical and emotional support from their partner and other children if the household, extended family, friends or religious organisations seem to provide little helpful support. In these circumstances, service supports are crucial if the needs of the child and family are to be met. Chapter 5 focused on the informal support experienced by families. This chapter focuses on family experiences of formal supports; supports provided by organisations expected to have expertise in helping families (Quinton 2004). For families with a child with severe disabilities, support organisations may include education, health, social services, voluntary sector and private sector organisations; therefore an important aspect of the family experience is how well these different organisations work together. This chapter also includes family experiences of supports sometimes described as semi-formal, such as parent groups (Quinton 2004). As with informal supports, formal supports can be described in several ways, including the source of support, the extent of support offered, the type of support offered and the helpfulness of the support offered. All the interviews in our study included sections designed to explore all these aspects of formal support in order to build a comprehensive picture of family experiences of formal supports.

This chapter starts by describing parental awareness and access to a wide range of health and welfare services for the child and family. Parents' views of their relationships with service professionals will also be outlined. More detail is then provided on a number of service supports shown in previous research to be crucial for families: special education services, short-term care/respite services, interpreting services, family support groups and keyworkers. The chapter also discusses services mentioned as needed but rarely received by parents in the Phase 1 and Phase 3 interviews. Next, the unmet needs of families are described, and the relationship between informal and formal support discussed. Finally, parents' plans, hopes and dreams for the future are outlined.

Awareness and access to service supports

Previous UK research has shown that South Asian families with a person with disabilities report high levels of awareness of general health and welfare support services such as the family doctor or dentist, but much lower awareness of specialist support services concerning the person with disabilities, such as speech therapy, psychology or psychiatry (Chamba *et al.* 1999; Hatton *et al.* 1998). South Asian parents with fluent English (Hatton *et al.* 1998) have been shown to have greater awareness of services. A lack of parental awareness has also been linked to relatively low access to family support services such as respite care and family support groups (Chamba *et al.* 1999; Hatton *et al.* 1998). There is also some evidence of inefficient targeting of services, with South Asian families with lower household income receiving fewer services (Hatton *et al.* 1998). Finally, South Asian families with a person with disabilities have identified culturally inappropriate services and racism as significant barriers to the uptake and continued use of services (Chamba *et al.* 1999; Hatton *et al.* 1998; Shah 1995).

To gain a general picture of parental awareness and use of a wide range of service supports, parents in the Phase 2 interviews completed the Client Service Receipt Interview (Personal Social Services Research Unit 1990). This has been used in previous research with UK South Asian families with a person with disabilities (Hatton *et al.* 1998), and asks parents about their awareness and uptake of 37 different support services in the past three months (Table 6.1).

Table 6.1 Number and percentage of parents reporting awareness and receipt of support services in the past three months: Phase 2

Service	aware of service	received service
1. Hospital in-patient	117 (86.0%)	28 (20.6%)
2. Hospital out-patient	122 (89.7%)	45 (33.1%)
3. Hospital day patient	120 (88.2%)	20 (14.7%)
4. GP	129 (94.9%)	93 (68.4%)
5. Psychiatrist	63 (46.3%)	3 (2.2%)
6. Other medical consultant	67 (49.3%)	10 (7.4%)
7. Dentist/oral hygienist	125 (91.9%)	64 (47.1%)
8. Chiropodist	51 (37.5%)	5 (3.7%)
9. Optician	119 (87.5%)	42 (30.9%)
10. Audiologist	49 (36.0%)	9 (6.6%)
11. Employment agency	53 (39.0%)	1 (0.7%)
12. District nurse	75 (55.1%)	7 (5.1%)
13. Community psychiatric nurse	46 (33.8%)	4 (2.9%)
14. Nursing auxiliary/assistant	36 (26.5%)	0 (0%)
15. Community learning disability nurse	41 (30.1%)	4 (2.9%)
16. Educational psychologist	47 (34.6%)	6 (4.4%)
17. Clinical psychologist	26 (19.1%)	2 (1.5%)
18. Speech therapist	96 (70.6%)	47 (34.6%)
19. Physiotherapist	93 (68.4%)	39 (28.7%)
20. Occupational therapist	43 (31.6%)	13 (9.6%)
21. Support worker	65 (47.8%)	24 (17.6%)
22. Volunteer visitor	37 (27.2%)	2 (1.5%)
23. Advocate	22 (16.2%)	0 (0%)
24. Additional support team	18 (13.2%)	0 (0%)

25. Respite care: short term	47 (34.6%)	7 (5.1%)
26. Respite care: long term	45 (33.1%)	1 (0.7%)
27. Transport	106 (77.9%)	105 (77.2%)
28. Health visitor	105 (77.2%)	19 (14.0%)
29. Genetic counsellor	30 (22.1%)	1 (0.7%)
30. Pre-school teacher	51 (37.5%)	6 (4.4%)
31. Social worker	115 (84.6%)	34 (25.0%)
32. Teacher	128 (94.1%)	115 (84.6%)
33. School doctor	123 (90.4%)	50 (36.8%)
34. School nurse	122 (89.7%)	51 (37.5%)
35. Hakim, Vaid/traditional healer	88 (64.7%)	2 (1.5%)
36. Religious healer	84 (61.8%)	2 (1.5%)
37. Child health clinic	82 (60.3%)	6 (4.4%)

In terms of parental awareness of services, Table 6.1 shows a similar pattern to that found in previous studies (Hatton *et al.* 1998). Parental awareness of general health and welfare services, such as the GP, dentist, hospital and social worker, was high. As education services are statutory, parental awareness of education services and other supports linked to them, such as transport and speech therapy, was also high. Awareness of specialist services not directly linked to the education system, such as clinical psychology and educational psychology, genetic counselling, respite care and advocacy services, was much lower.

Table 6.1 also shows that uptake of service supports was generally very low, particularly when taking into account the many and complex support needs of the children. Only education, transport and GP services were reported by more than half of parents as being used in the past three months. Where services had been received, the vast majority of parents reported that the service was sufficient for their needs and helpful to them.

There were several differences between ethnic groups in terms of parental awareness and uptake of services. In terms of parental awareness of services, with the exception of hospital services Indian parents generally reported higher levels of awareness than Bangladeshi parents, who in turn reported higher levels of service awareness than Pakistani parents. This pattern of service awareness was present for 20 of the 37 formal and semi-formal service supports listed. Differences in service uptake between ethnic groups were much fewer and less dramatic, possibly due to the relatively low levels of service uptake across all ethnic groups. Here again, with the exception of Bangladeshi families receiving more transport services, Indian families were more likely to receive five different types of service support (chiropodist, optician, community learning disabilities nurse, speech therapist, child health clinic). Indian parents reported the greatest overall awareness of services and Pakistani parents reported the lowest overall awareness of services, although there was no difference between ethnic groups in overall service uptake.

We also examined differences in service awareness and uptake according to whether parents were fluent in the English language. Parents fluent in English were more likely to be aware of 15 out of the 37 formal supports listed. However, parental English language use was only linked to the family receiving four services (GP, employment agency, district nurse, short-term care/respite care). Overall, greater parental awareness of services was linked to parents speaking, reading and writing English. In contrast, greater overall service uptake was not linked to English language use.

For parents in the Phase 1 interviews, any service support outside school hours was appreciated, although these services were rare.

[Name of support worker] comes and she helps me with the housework. And then there's another person who does a few days in the evenings... She takes him out in the car for an hour and he enjoys that.

Amani

The help that I get the most is that a nurse comes two nights a week so I can have a rest. She comes from 10pm till 6am, apart from that I do not get any other help.

Farida

Home help is the most important need I would say, because all the pressure falls on the mother. She has to care for all the family and do the housework as well. So if there was some help in the house it would be a great help... Three times a week, hoovering and ironing.

Ayesha

A lack of parental awareness of services (cited by 93.8% of parents) and language issues (lack of interpreting services, cited by 75.0% of parents) were cited by parents in the Phase 2 interviews as major reasons why South Asian families with a child with disabilities did not use services. However, as we have seen, parental awareness and good communication did not in themselves guarantee access to services. Indeed, parents also cited culturally inadequate and inappropriate services (71.8% of parents) and discrimination in services (39.8% of parents) as major reasons for services not being used.

A lack of cultural awareness and racism were also cited by some Phase 1 parents as reasons for not gaining access to or continuing to use services.

> What I think is that we've been ignored because I come from the ethnic minority.
>
> *Jabir*

> I think it's not just me 'cos a lot of other Asian people and a lot of Black people tend to think when you've got these English doctors they're not bothered. 'Oh no, it's an Asian. Never mind I'll see to one of our own.' … They're not bothered.
>
> *Nasreen*

> I told the health visitor that I am having problems with controlling Nadia. She contacted the community support team again and they sent a person, English… He used to come and observe Nadia and then advise… I did not feel comfortable with him being there. I asked him to stop coming as he was male and Nadia was a girl. Also he did not understand the system in our families.
>
> *Henna*

Some parents in the Phase 3 interviews, however, expressed the view that South Asian professionals could be unhelpful or unsympathetic.

> Sometimes I have spoken to Asian staff and doctors and they have not spoken to me in Punjabi, even though they can see that I find it a problem to speak English. I cannot explain myself deeply in English… Even now I feel angry at the Asian doctors as they have been very arrogant with me.
>
> *Zareena*

> Yes, I had problems with Asian staff at the children's hospital. The doctor seemed to think very highly of herself and was very arrogant towards me. I have found Asians to be more arrogant and English staff to be more humble.
>
> *Akhmal*

Helpfulness of service supports

Using the Client Service Receipt Interview (see above), we asked parents in the Phase 2 interviews to nominate the most helpful and least helpful service they had received. Of course, services can only be nominated as helpful or otherwise if they have been used by parents, therefore limiting the potential range of responses. The most helpful services nominated by at least ten parents were: teacher or school (26.5%); GP, doctor or consultant (16.2%); and social worker (11.8%). Only social workers (11.8%) and GP, doctor or consultant (7.4%) were nominated by ten or more parents as the most unhelpful service. It is clear that parents strongly value education services, whereas parents' experiences of other services such as GPs or social workers is extremely diverse, receiving nominations for both most helpful and least helpful service. For example, parents in the Phase 3 interviews reported very diverse experiences of social workers.

> Social workers are very helpful for certain things such as giving information, getting facilities and applying for benefits.
>
> *Zora*

> They would just talk and I felt that I had to be careful with them. I have heard cases where social workers have disrupted homes or taken the child away.
>
> *Zareena*

> They have little time, too much paperwork and no time to visit.
>
> *Huda*

> It can be hard getting in touch as they are always out and by the time they get in touch with you, you have solved the problem.
>
> *Jabir*

> They will give you professional advice but they won't touch you emotionally... The school teachers will always listen to you even if it's just for emotional support, but social workers are too professional and too cold.
>
> *Henna*

We also asked parents in the Phase 2 interviews about the availability and helpfulness of a range of service supports, using the Family Support Scale (Dunst *et al.* 1998) completed by Phase 2 parents. Parents found school services, professional helpers and GP support particularly helpful, with more diversity of opinion concerning professional agencies. Even where other supports such as parent groups, social clubs and early intervention schemes were available, they were rated as less helpful by parents. In terms of availability and helpfulness, schools, professional helpers and GPs were at similar levels to the support received from parents' partners, children and parents' parents (see Chapter 5).

Overall, most parents in the Phase 2 interviews were generally quite satisfied (76.3%) with the services they received, with a small number very satisfied (3.8%) and a significant minority not satisfied with services (19.1%). These are similar levels of satisfaction to those reported by parents in the Chamba *et al.* (1999) study.

A strong feature of our study was to gain practical ideas for improving services. As well as asking parents about how specific services could be improved (see later in this chapter), we also asked parents for their ideas about improving support services generally. In our study, information and cultural issues came to the fore. Almost all parents in the interviews wanted more information about services in relevant languages (91%), culturally sensitive services (89%) and more South Asian staff throughout services (82%). Most parents also wanted services for the child to be integrated with children without disabilities (84%), with only a very small minority of parents (2%) preferring segregated services.

According to parents in the Phase 1 interviews, several aspects of service supports influenced their helpfulness, which in turn could influence parental decisions about whether to use certain services. For example, service supports viewed as insufficient or unreliable were viewed as actively unhelpful by parents, and sometimes seen as worse than having no service support at all. Communication barriers also led to parental frustrations at not being able to maximise the helpfulness of the service supports they received.

We also need more Asian doctors as I have a three or four hour wait.

Shaziza

At this moment I do have some help in the morning because [support worker] helps with changing him in the mornings, but I look after him for the rest of the day... She only helps me a little.

Zora

A support worker did come in the mornings to help get Shahid ready for school, but she rarely came and so I said I was OK doing it myself.

Faiza

I used to get a support worker coming, but the problem was that I could not explain to her about my problems fully. Anyhow, I did not get the levels of help needed.

Henna

He's [child with disabilities] got a whole load of problems just with that tiny bit of chromosome missing. That is very hard for us to accept... We've explained to them [consultants] but they don't want to know. They don't explain... They don't sit down you know. They'll tell you things... And they come off with all this and you don't understand. You say will you explain to us... Sayed's made a lot of progress, but the doctor told us. They told us he was zilch, nothing, a vegetable... I don't take him to see the doctors down at the hospital any more.

Nasreen

For many Phase 1 parents, service supports lacked an emotional support dimension. This was particularly distressing for parents who did not receive emotional support from informal sources, such as partners, extended family or friends.

Sometimes you think 'Well what about me?' I don't get any support. I don't have a mum to say 'Well look can I have a weekend to myself and can you have him?' I've tried respite but you don't get any help... I was having a nervous breakdown and it was his birthday and his teacher actually took him from school to keep him for the night because I was not feeling all right in myself [upset] you know... It's normal for us to feel down, have down days when we're down and fed up you know. Then we have our days when we feel strong enough to say 'Well I'll be all right, I'll cope' you know, but I don't feel that I really do get that emotional support that I needed ever since he was born. And every time I've wanted to look where the support is, there have just been false promises.

Shahina

Relationships with professionals and problems with services

Parents in the Phase 2 interviews were asked about their relationship with professionals, using questions in Chamba *et al.* (1999) derived from Laybourn and Hill (1991). According to Laybourn and Hill (1991), one form of relationship, collaboration between parents and professionals, is positive, with other forms of relationship being negative. The percentage of parents reporting different forms of relationships with professionals is listed below.

Table 6.2 Percentage of parents reporting different forms of relationships	
Collaboration: parents and professionals respect each other, recognise their respective contribution and act as equals	42.7%
Coexistence: parents and professionals do not interfere with each other	32.8%
Confusion: respective roles are unclear	17.6%
Colonisation: professionals take over	4.4%
Conflict: parents and professionals have contrasting objectives	2.3%

Less than half the parents in our study reported collaborative relationships with professionals, compared to over half the parents in the Chamba *et al.* (1999) study. In contrast to the parents in Chamba *et al.* (1999), in our study Pakistani parents were less likely than Indian and Bangladeshi parents to report collaborative relationships with professionals. English language use was not linked to parents reporting a collaborative relationship with professionals.

Again using questions from Chamba *et al.* (1999), parents in the Phase 2 interviews were asked whether they experienced 17 different problems with services. We reduced these 17 problems into four scales: lack of confidence in professionals; having to fight to get services; inconvenient hospital services; and difficult communication with services.

Overall, over 80 per cent of parents reported that they had problems with the length of time it took to get services organised (87%), not knowing which services were available (82%) and not knowing where to get information (81%). A large majority of parents also reported having to fight to get services (75%), services being reduced or withdrawn (74%) and problems with having to wait too long at the hospital (73%). These problems were generally similar to those reported by Chamba *et al.* (1999) for parents across ethnic groups and also by Beresford (1995) with largely White parents. It is also worth noting that a relatively small number of parents reported problems with not being able to attend appointments with their partner (21%), not liking the number of professionals visiting the home (15%) and professionals putting pressure on parents to carry out treatments with the child (14%).

Again similarly to the Chamba *et al.* (1999) study, there were several differences across ethnic groups in the reporting of problems with services, with Bangladeshi parents reporting fewer problems in 5 out of 17 specific problems (not knowing where to go for information; having to fight for everything the child needs; having to wait a long time at the hospital; having to wait a long time between visits or appointments; the service not understanding the parent's culture or religion) and two out of four scales (lack of confidence in professionals and inconvenient hospital services). Indian parents were more likely to report problems with professionals not understanding their culture or religion and more problems in communicating with services. Chamba *et al.* (1999) argue that, as with parental perceptions of the adequacy of information about services, the reports of Bangladeshi parents may be a function of low expectations rather than better-quality service support. Not speaking, reading or writing English was also linked to more problems with the scale of having to fight to get services.

Parents in the Phase 1 interviews reported struggles with professionals about the care of their child that sometimes continued for years. This resulted in delays in service support, inappropriate services being provided and parental frustration and lack of confidence in professionals.

I was very annoyed when the doctor first told me about the disability, because they had done an assessment at the hospital and it was decided that he should go to a special school right from the first day but I was not informed about it. And the Education Department did have an assessment when he was 1½ years old but when I was told he was 4. And then I had an argument with the Education Department. Even then they didn't send him to a special school. They left him in a mainstream school and they gave him a support teacher, a special teacher. They used to come in for certain days in the week… I went in there on a parents evening. I asked the teacher. I said 'How's Sharukh doing?' She just said 'Nothing to do with me… I've no time for him. I've got so many other children to look after. He just comes to school. He does what he wants and he can sit down, he can walk, he can talk, whatever he wants. Whatever education he's getting is when the special teacher comes from the Education Department for a couple of hours a week'. So I went to the Education Department and just told them 'Before the new term starts he should be in a special school and not in this school any more'. They said, 'No we can't do that'… He settled down there [special school] very quickly but I had to fight for it, to send him to a special school.

Jabir [English speaker]

When the social worker came she completed the [benefit] forms and took them. The forms were five to six weeks late. So they started the claim from the 12th of February rather than the earlier date. So I went to the advice bureau yesterday. They have an Asian person there and they sorted it out. I need this type of help as I'm not educated myself… The weeks pass by and are wasted in this way. My problem is that there is no one to complete forms for me. There is also no one to talk for me. Now the Pakistani girl who works part time, she is free every Monday. If she becomes ill or some work comes up she won't be there on Monday. If I go then I become even more late by a week. These are things that I can't do.

Shaziza

Even my social workers didn't know what facilities were available for people with learning disabilities. There was nothing on hand at the hospital or the social workers hadn't got time. There was nothing that said that there was any respite care available or anything at all… And it wasn't until I was sat talking to my health visitor… I said 'I'm washing my hands after everything I touch and I'm tidying and I've got to the extent where I'm obsessed now'…and then it came to it that I nearly committed suicide… When I was ready to be discharged the people in the hospital where I had the nervous breakdown they got in contact with the respite care and services for me [upset]. Why couldn't that have been done before?

Firdaus

[We cannot take child with disabilities out because] his wheelchair is too small. We've applied for another one but they just don't seem to listen…it has been an age since we have been telling them about the chair, and he cannot sit in it as his head drops to one side… A lady from the social services also came and said that she will help with a chair but she hasn't been back.

Faiza

Sayed's always had a problem with constipation. The doctors have always ignored it… He has a hernia which he had to have an operation on… The doctors have been ignoring it for the past three and a half years. I explained properly to her [paediatrician] and she sorted it out…

And all it was was changing a bottle of medicine from one to another. If the consultant can't even be bothered to do that what's the point of me wasting my time, wasting my son's time... Every time we were massaging [name of child]'s stomach for those two years we were damaging him.

Nasreen

My husband has to take time off work to look after the other children while I take Iman to the doctor or hospital. Obviously I have to take her to the hospital even if I end up spending the whole day there.

Azra

At that time we were not used to it [the child's disabilities]. I know more now. I used to go to hospitals on buses and it would be very difficult to take him with me. I had to pick him up and change two buses to go to the children's hospital... I became very tired and got back pain.

Zora

At first I did not understand what to do. When she became difficult to control I felt that I needed help. Someone to tell me how to handle her... I used to get frustrated that I cannot do what is best for her. I would get angry at her for doing something wrong but then think to myself that she does not understand my anger. I had no confidence. I would sit and cry... I used to use ordinary nappies for her which were too small. Then I was told that I could get special nappies for her... I think she was 5 or 6 years old.

Henna

At the moment she [child with disabilities] especially needs a lot of care...she's 18 and I think she's finishing [school] this summer. So she will be all the time at home. So mainly we will need help. Somebody who can provide home service... I asked this school to provide me some sort of service which can help my wife, but there again we've got a lot of problems. We're Asians, Bengalis. Somebody comes from a different culture. It is hard for my wife. She doesn't understand English and it's hard for her to make someone understand... I don't mind to be honest, but if we get some of our own culture people it's a lot better and I feel better...[the advantages would be] my wife can talk. The language problem. Plus they can come and understand what sort of problems she's facing. Mainly the cultural ways, because I can feel for other [Bengali/South Asian] people how they're suffering, but with different cultures there's difficulties they will take it how they have been working on it. 'Cos one time I have been asked at school, because my daughter is going to an adult service, do I mind if her nappy is changed by a male rather than a female. This is a difficult one, she's 18.

Arslan

I asked my health visitor that over the weekend, if she could arrange for my daughters [two daughters with disabilities] to go swimming for only one hour if not more. It will be a change for them. I and my daughters would be happy. She said you have to wait a long time, there is a two-year waiting list. I told her that is too long. They can't even help me that much.

Azra

Some parents in the Phase 1 interviews also reported that service professionals (other than special education services) often could not cope with their child's disabilities, resulting in support services that were actively unhelpful and often discontinued.

The social worker had arranged for a nurse to come and take care of her [child with disabilities] at night time. I thought that person was not appropriate. Whenever she [child with disabilities] had a problem that person would wake me up straight away. I could not go to sleep anyway. Whenever I did fall asleep she would wake me up to tell me that she has this problem then I would have to give her the treatment myself.

Farida

Six weeks are just a headache again… I needed Yusuf to go to a nursery or playgroups where he will have that care taken and they just give you a list of all these care places and summer schemes and all this, but it's about 50-odd children there with two carers. And they can't give him that one to one that he needs. So then they phone up after half an hour and say 'Well look he needs more attention and we can't give it him. So basically will you come and stay with him?' So what's the point? So there's nothing really out there. And he's been on the respite list now for the last two to three years. Not a thing.

Shahina

Education services

As has been reported throughout this chapter, education services seemed to be the most crucial ongoing service for families. As we have seen, the vast majority of parents were aware of and currently receiving special education services. Parents also reported education services overall as the most helpful source of support of any source of informal, semi-formal or formal support, although parental understanding of the SEN statementing process was limited. Parents in all interview phases were asked in more detail about their experience of education services.

Almost all the children with severe learning disabilities were reported by parents in the Phase 2 interviews to be in special schools for children with severe learning difficulties (83.8%), with a small minority of children being placed in a mainstream school (4.4%). Just over half the pre school-age children (5.1% of the total) were in a nursery, while the remainder (3.7% of the total) were not receiving any education services. Finally, a small number of children (2.9%) were reported by parents as having recently left special education provision.

We asked those parents in the Phase 2 interviews with children at school for their opinions about 12 different aspects of the school service, using questions from Chamba et al. (1999). Parents were generally positive about the facilities offered by schools, although there was considerable diversity of opinion among parents. The vast majority of parents felt it was at least somewhat true that their child was progressing well (93%) and enjoying school (96%), that the school was well-equipped (91%) and the school kept parents informed (69% had discussed their child with the school in the past month). In addition, only a small minority of parents felt it was very true that the school was not able to cope with the child (8%) and did not meet the child's needs (9%), and that there were no other children of the same culture in the school (5%). However, there were some problems with school services reported by parents. Many parents reported that it was at least somewhat true that there was no education at the school in relevant Asian languages (79%) and not enough speech therapy/physiotherapy at the school (47%), the same factors reported as a problem by parents in the Chamba et al. (1999) study.

There were very few differences between ethnic groups in parental opinions about school services. Indian parents were more likely to report that their child was not at their preferred school and that the school did not understand their child compared to Pakistani and particularly Bangladeshi families, again possibly partly a function of differences in parental expectations.

For parents in the Phase 2 interviews, the biggest areas for improvement in education services concerned meeting the cultural and religious needs of their child, including staff being sensitive to the child's cultural needs (81% of parents endorsed this), employing South Asian staff within the school (63%

of parents), the school providing appropriate food (63% of parents) and the school engaging children in culture-related activities (62% of parents). Fewer parents (25%) wanted single-sex schools for their child; this was more likely among parents of girls although it was not a view exclusively held by them. In addition, this was the only area of improvement where there was a difference between ethnic groups, with Indian parents less likely to want a single-sex school compared to parents from other ethnic groups.

Almost all the parents in the Phase 1 interviews were very satisfied with the special school service their child with severe learning disabilities was receiving. Some parents contrasted the extra support provided by the special school compared to mainstream education services.

> We were apprehensive about sending Faizal to a special school as Asian people talk about why a child goes to a special school. So we arranged for a nursery. After a year they said they could not provide the proper facilities for him. Then they arranged for the special school. We never had any problems with the school. Normal schools do not have the facilities for special needs children. They have less children in a class in a special school so the children get looked after better, secondly he gets help with his speech. Also he previously had trouble speaking but since he started school it has helped him a lot and now not just us but the rest of the members of our family can understand him.
>
> *Duaa*

> She goes to special school so that parents can get help. At school they try their best [to meet the child's special needs]. She can also walk in the school hall by using a special frame... Her legs get a lot of exercise... When she is at school I get a break... I think if there was no school I would go mad running after them all day.
>
> *Azra*

Many parents reported that their children actively enjoyed school, and were benefiting from the substantial support provided.

> She sees more people. The teachers take a bit more time with lessons and feeding.
>
> *Arslan*

> He goes there and gets into the physio side...and they give him aromatherapy, swimming in water. And it gets him away from the house.

A different environment, it's good. I couldn't be there all the time. I couldn't care for him at home as well.

Firdaus

He is more happy at school. Even if he has a bit of a cold he will want to go to school.

Duaa

They [two children with disabilities] are happy with school. They like music, exercise, swimming baths and seeing different people. They get bored at home and cry a lot. They have more open space at the school.

Zora

He cannot see but I think he reacts to light and movement. He likes that and he enjoys being with the other children... He listens to the other children shouting or talking and then he will also try and speak out.

Faiza

[Child with disabilities enjoys] talking [laughs]. He likes drawing but he just draws round circles like this [indicates with hand]. And he likes talking a lot with the teachers. 'Where did you go? Why were you ill?' or 'How did that happen?' He wants to talk to people all the time.

Zareena

She is happy. She always smiles when she is taken out. She will look everywhere and listen to what is going on. She likes her school trips. I also think that when she goes out she doesn't become bored. She went to a trip yesterday and came back in the evening. She is very happy.

Huda

Many parents also mentioned that the special school acted as a form of respite service for them, giving parents a break free from worry, as parents were confident that the school was looking after their child properly.

The school service makes my life easier, if there wasn't this school service then my life wouldn't be very good... It doesn't seem to me that anything would help me more than this. To be honest I'm not saying this because I have to say it as my child goes there. I'm very happy with the school. In fact whichever [special] school I've dealt with up till now I haven't felt unhappy. And the staff especially seem very welcoming. I feel at home. I don't know if anyone has ever felt unhappy about the school but I'm happy.

Zareena

he's [child with disabilities] got a lovely school… They've all been very considerate when I've felt a bit down.

Shahina

During the day time when he's [child with disabilities] at school I'll quickly do the house chores and then go shopping or go visiting relatives. Then I don't have to worry about him. But if he's at home all day [at weekends] then I'm working in with him giving him his drinks, feeding him, changing him…and obviously I'm just working my day all round him…it [school] gives us a rest and a break as well.

Firdaus

When she is at school I get a break. If she [child with disabilities] was to stay at home all the time I would get very tired. So the school helps me very much… When they [two daughters with disability] are at home I worry. I don't go out or manage to do anything…and also [when they're at school] if there is someone ill or there are any other problems in the family then I can go out and visit them during the day. It's easy for me.

Huda

At first I would not send her [child with disabilities] to school in this condition because she needs tube feeding and she is in pain. She has various problems and that is why I thought 'What is the point of sending her?', but they said it will be better for me if they look after her during the day and I look after her during the night. The staff at school are all so nice.

Farida

Schools were generally felt by parents to be responsive to their concerns, although schools rarely made arrangements to meet children's cultural or religious needs.

The thing is what annoyed me was that when he [child with disabilities] got a phobia of animals see. The teacher bringing a dog into the school and at times the dog got into the school hall…you know that's most upsetting for me. But when I had a calm word with them I was assured that whenever he [child] goes into that place the dog is not there… I'm happy because Sharukh never made a complaint after that. So that means he's satisfied [laughs].

Jabir

At the school I told them to be careful and that's how they have been. I told her teacher that Humaria is older now and she has fits, so her teacher should be a woman. Then they had a woman teacher for her.

Shaziza

I told the school to give her [child with disabilities] only halal food. Sometimes she won't even have mashed potato and they will go and get chips for her from the chip shop.

Huda

A minority of Phase 1 parents reported dissatisfaction with special school services, as they felt that their child with disabilities was receiving a poor standard of care. One parent also reported dissatisfaction at the lack of choice concerning education services.

I don't feel that he's happy there [school]... The teachers though say he is happy and well there. They help him a lot but Harron is not happy with other people as he is with me, because he's with me all the time.

Roshni

Because he [child with disabilities] doesn't talk, he's had a lot of problems at school. He's come home and he's got a lot of marks on his face and body...and they [teachers] deny he's, anything's happened at school. They all try to shift the blame on 'Oh, he must have done it at home. Oh, he's done it on the minibus'. And well for a fact I know he's not done it at home, he's not done it on the minibus. I know it's happened at school... I've seen things happen [upset]. I've been into school... The physios had this wedge thing for him because his chest muscles are quite weak... He's on this wedge. He's got a whole load of tissues on the floor 'cos he had a cold...all these tissues on the floor to catch his nose so the carpet wouldn't get dirty... I was just like walking into school [unannounced]... And as soon as I walked into the classroom you've got three teachers running around to get a tissue to clean his nose.

Nasreen

The only problem was that in my first house I had steps leading up to the front door. And sometimes when the school bus would pick up Shahid they would help with taking him down the steps. However, once or twice a particular lady would come and I said to her 'I have difficulty with the stairs and could you help me by holding one side of the wheelchair'. She said 'No, that's not my job'. She just became angry and watched me do it alone… After that another lady would come with the school bus and she would help or the driver would help. He was very nice and would come and offer to help.

Faiza

They just said 'This is the best school'. We wanted that if she has to attend special school it should be where there are less disabled children than in this school. At this school there were children with mental and physical disabilities, but Nadia did not suffer from any of these. But after going to this school she began to behave in a strange way…she was copying. This upsets us all. We asked if there was another school, but were told that there was no other school. We were not given any choice.

Henna

Special schools were also very frequently a point of access and a site for the child to receive a range of other service supports, such as physiotherapy and speech therapy.

I had no confidence. I would sit and cry. Then the school gave me the number to contact the community support team and said that they can help if I have any problems. I used to use ordinary nappies for her, then I was told that I could get special nappies for her.

Henna

I don't take him to see any of the doctors down at the hospital any more [due to a past history of problems with the consultant there]… He [child with disabilities] just has one community paediatrician and she's really helped me a lot. Well she helped Sayed a lot with a lot of the problems that he's had. I'll just see her [paediatrician] at school if I have any problems, or I'll just let the school know that I want to see her and she'll arrange to see him.

Nasreen

Parents in the Phase 1 interviews had diverse views of the helpfulness of physiotherapy services, with some expressing benefits and others reporting some concerns.

At this school I'd say the physios aren't [helpful]. They're not really bothered… The physio at school she's a nice friendly person but she's not really [nice]. Sayed hasn't really made much progress with them [compared to the previous school].

Nasreen

I feel a bit awkward about the physio. What the physio does, the child cannot say anything. If he had the ability to speak then he could do whatever he is told to do. Sometimes he does not want to do an activity, but he is made to do it with difficulty... The physio does not have any sympathy for him. OK you make him do it once. If he does not want to do it again then leave it, but the physio does not agree to that.

Mariah

For many parents, the special school was their only significant source of support, with parents receiving very little support during the school holidays.

I don't get any other help apart from that she goes to school. Nobody helps me to take her out. In the six weeks holidays parents need a lot of help but we don't get any help of this sort. I would like help to take her out for a short time. I can't even take out my other children during the six weeks holidays because I'm taking care of the two girls [with disabilities].

Azra

We need something more for these children to have a social life after school. Somewhere they can go. And more in the holidays like playgroups, more of them. It would benefit the children because they would be less bored and they would be mixing with people and still have their minds occupied...[and her other daughter] she'd have her freedom then, because she could do her own thing.

Shahina

Short-term care/respite care

As reported earlier in this chapter, only a minority of parents in the Phase 2 interviews were aware of respite care services, and very few had received respite care for their child in the past three months. This finding is similar to previous UK studies of South Asian families with a child or adult with learning disabilities (Chamba *et al.* 1999; Hatton *et al.* 1998). Only 32 per cent of parents in the Phase 2 interviews reported getting enough breaks from caring for their child; these breaks were most likely to be provided by unpaid family members (34% of parents) or playschemes in the school holidays (17% of parents) rather than respite services.

Very few parents in the Phase 2 interviews (10%) reported receiving respite care services of any kind and this was mostly in specialist respite centres managed by social services. Of this small number of parents, 29 per cent of them reported having to pay for respite care. Less than half the parents (43%) reported that the respite service had made arrangements to meet the child's cultural and religious needs.

Most parents who were aware of respite services but not using them reported choosing not to use respite, similarly to previous UK research finding significant parental concerns about the quality of respite services across a range of ethnic groups (Beresford 1995; Chamba *et al.* 1999; Hatton *et al.* 1998). The most common reasons reported by parents aware of respite services for not using them included the child not liking the respite service (73% of relevant parents), parental concerns about abuse (68% of parents) and respite services providing culturally inappropriate ways of caring (59% of parents).

Despite these concerns, once Phase 2 parents had become aware of respite services through the interview procedure, almost half (46%) reported that they wanted to receive some form of respite service for their child and themselves. Parental suggestions for improving respite care services focused on raising parental awareness of services (58%), raising service awareness of how to provide culturally appropriate services (58%), more easily accessible services (56%), having staff who know the child well (56%), easy availability of interpreters (54%), same-sex respite carers (45%), family-based respite services with families from the same ethnic group (37%) and same-ethnic group respite carers (35%). Parental opinions concerning the importance of having South Asian staff within respite services were diverse. Almost half thought this was important or very important (46%), but almost as many parents were not bothered or thought this was not important (39%).

Some parents in the Phase 1 and Phase 3 interviews expressed a need for culturally sensitive respite care services, sometimes with feelings of guilt about wanting to spend some time away from their child.

> Carers feel guilty about using breaks services and need convincing that they are not shifting the responsibility on to others. They need to be told that they need a break in order to provide better care of their child.
>
> *Akhmal*

> We need a centre to give us a short break from Humaria's behaviour problems and to assess her problems and treatment needs. We also need understanding doctors to control her behaviour and a service where boys and girls are separate.
>
> *Shaziza*

Yes, if I have a baby and maybe need to stay in hospital for a day or two and if they [respite care] could look after Iman it would be really helpful. Her nappies need to be changed and I personally would not like her father to change her nappy.

Azra

For the first five years I would not use it because I felt guilty with somebody else looking after my child. I felt it was my responsibility and wondered 'Will someone else take care of my child well?' But obviously you need that break. Carers need to be encouraged and reassured that the child needs help and support for your sake. If you're run down you won't be able to take care of the child. At first I did not like using it, but now I have experienced it and I look forward to it now.

Firdaus

You know I just long for a time when I think 'God, a week. I can go away for a week'. 'Cos in 11 years I have not had a week's break from him and I so desperately need that, but there is no one there who I think is going to take him for a week. And I feel really guilty about that... He's had 11 years of my life and I've not come to these decisions overnight... And I do talk to a lot of people who've said 'It's all right to feel the way you're feeling'.

Shahina

Where respite care was received, it could be a highly valued support for parents. Although parents reported that the amount of respite care was often insufficient, some parents reported that respite care services did take account of the cultural and religious needs of their child.

Since January Umber goes every Monday and stays one night. It gives my wife a little bit of a break [respite service provides halal food and a female carer]... I work so I am out but at least one day it releases the pressure on her [wife]. It is better for her especially and we think it's better for the family as well. We could do with a few days more.

Arslan

One good thing is that he goes to school and the other is we've been introduced to respite care, which is one night in a fortnight where he goes and I don't think that's enough. It's not enough but they've got other people on the waiting list and it's got to be shared equally...the service itself is brilliant.

Firdaus

I told them [respite care] that Irfan is Muslim and eats halal food so they arrange accordingly.

Samaya

They're [respite care] made aware of how we look after her and sort of mimic that.

Akhmal

However, parents also reported a number of problems with respite care services. These included delays in accessing respite care, the lack of flexibility in accessing respite care at short notice, and a lack of parental confidence in respite care services to look after their child.

Well we asked for respite care before my youngest daughter was born and they contacted us about eight, nine months later and then you know there was no need. I wanted respite care while my wife went into hospital, but they were slow in replying and I made them aware of that. And the social services blamed it on lack of resources and total excuses.

Akhmal

And the [respite] service doesn't provide like say we've got something that happens in the family. Like er you know in our culture when like there's a death in the family and all the families have to come round and all at once. There's nowhere I can take him [child with disabilities]... I'm struggling. That I've got nowhere I can take him at short notice.

Firdaus

I put a cloth over myself because he spurts it [food] out and I sit down and I feed him. It's hard. So I wouldn't use respite for that reason. If it was an emergency and could not be helped then I would use it... [My wish would be] halal food the way we cook it. And I would want them to clean Shahid the way that I clean him.

Faiza

I do not wish to use respite care as both my children became ill there. I have also seen abuse on TV towards these children where the child was beaten up and starved. The staff should be more responsible and cautious.

Zora

One parent in the Phase 1 interviews had used family-based respite care, but its lack of predictability and short duration limited its usefulness. Other parents in the Phase 3 interviews would prefer family-based respite care.

> You know she was gonna like have Yusuf for ever [laughs], because it's such a big deal somebody saying 'I'm gonna have him on Friday night you know and I'll bring him back on Sunday', and you think 'Wow, all that time for me'. And basically it never worked out and I never expected it not to... The respite care let me down... I appreciate what I have but it's nothing long term. It's nothing stable for me to look forward to.
>
> *Shahina*

> We would be concerned about abuse as you don't have the opportunity to get to know all the people in the home. The child has to keep on adapting to other rules with different people...the family respite would be better as when you know someone you feel more secure.
>
> *Akram*

> I would use respite firstly if somebody was familiar to you and your child through previous contact. Respite care seems such a big deal. I'd feel it was my responsibility and I'd feel guilty. I'd worry about her care. She might be suffering. Unless I know that she will be looked after properly I will not use the service. You hear so many bad things on the media. Maybe an Asian family respite would be more reassuring than a centre as you can get to know and gain confidence in the family.
>
> *Henna*

> I would also like to have night support from a family placement respite scheme. It is better than other respite care, as it is easier and more reassuring to give your child to a couple who you will have a chance to build a relationship with.
>
> *Roshni*

In the absence of dedicated respite care services, some parents in the Phase 1 interviews reported their child using hospital services at times of crisis, although the experience of hospital services could reduce parental confidence in the capacity of respite services to care for their child.

> At present Shabir is just about all right. He is in hospital now, because his mother is ill. For her illness they have sent him to hospital for a week.
>
> *Mariah*

No [I would not like respite care] because when Shahid goes to hospital when he's ill, the nurses they cannot feed him. And so they leave him and wait for me to come and feed him. So if he's left like that without eating for a couple of days he will probably die won't he?

Faiza

Interpreting services

As has been reported in Chapter 2, most parents in our study did not speak, read or write English. We have also seen throughout the earlier chapters that communication barriers caused by a reliance on English use within services are linked to a lack of parental understanding of their child's disability, and a lack of parental awareness and uptake of services. In these circumstances, interpreting services can play a crucial role in improving family access to services. As Chamba *et al.* (1999) state, the role of an interpreter is highly skilled, requiring not only linguistic skills, but also specialist knowledge and sensitivity to parental feelings.

Although most of the parents in the Phase 2 interviews (65%) reported needing an interpreter, a minority (40%) reported having been provided with an interpreter by professionals. Interpreting services were highly valued by those parents who had received them, particularly in terms of allowing parents to say what they wanted (68%), parents not having to rely on family or friends to interpret (66%) and interpreters ensuring confidentiality from family or friends (55%). However, a substantial minority of parents reported negative experiences with interpreting services, such as their taking too long to arrange (29%), interpreters not knowing anything about disability (16%) and interpreters not being sympathetic (13%). A small number of parents reported problems with interpreters breaking confidentiality (7%), not speaking the relevant dialect (7%), being inaccurate (5%) or using difficult language (5%). Parents in our study appeared to rate interpreting services more highly than parents in the Chamba *et al.* (1999) study; also in contrast to Chamba *et al.* (1999) there were no differences between ethnic groups.

In the absence of a professional interpreter, parents relied mainly on their spouse or partner (29% of parents) or another child in the household (20%), with occasional support from extended family members (7%).

Few parents in the Phase 1 and Phase 3 interviews reported using an interpreter. Although interpreters were valued where they had been provided, they were felt to not always be sharing everything. Parents emphasised the need for interpreters to be available when needed, particularly in health services during emergencies, and to have an understanding of disability issues. One parent also pointed out the Catch-22 position that it was impossible to ask for an interpreter if nobody in the service understood the parents' language.

> I am happy with my experiences of interpreters and have easy access to her. She contacts me herself and asks me if I need any help and I can arrange appointments for her to visit me with my English health visitor.
>
> *Zakiya*

> The benefits I've had from social services are actually great, because I've had to go abroad once or twice and because my wife cannot speak good English... They've been taking Sharukh down to see the doctor and my wife and explained to them. Because they've been involved for the past few years they know nearly everything, see... I would say that it didn't make me get worried when I was abroad.
>
> *Jabir*

> The social worker brings their interpreter with them and she is Pakistani and she is very nice. She has fought for a few things and even with the things that I did not know she tells me that I need these things and they need to be given to me.
>
> *Farida*

> The interpreter would not completely explain to me what the teachers had said to me. The interpreter would select what was said to rush things and I was not happy as I was not able to explain all my feelings to the teachers.
>
> *Zareena*

> They should have an interpreter available at the hospital all the time, without the need for an appointment, otherwise you go away feeling that there was nobody there when you needed the help. They should also have interpreters who are experienced with learning disability.
>
> *Firdaus*

> I need an Asian person to be able to contact and someone who will go to the hospital with me. Or alternatively, they should have interpreters available at all times in the emergency department as that is a more urgent need.
>
> *Shaziza*

There should be an interpreter there [in hospital]. A good one. These days some of them don't explain everything. They just tell you key things. You want to and need to know more... They should themselves provide families with an interpreter as families don't know how to ask for one if they cannot speak English.

Henna

Family support groups

Support groups are a potentially useful source of information, and practical and emotional support for families with a child with disabilities from minority ethnic groups (Mir *et al.* 2001). However, our study, as in previous UK studies, has found low rates of parental awareness and uptake of support groups compared to White families (Beresford 1995; Chamba *et al.* 1999). Only 19 per cent of parents in the Phase 2 interviews reported belonging to a support group. No Bangladeshi parents belonged to a support group, compared to 39 per cent of Indian parents and 15 per cent of Pakistani parents.

Parents who did attend support groups reported their helpfulness to be limited, with their functions largely concerning information about local services (91% of those attending), benefits (81%), the child's condition (75%) and planning for the future (72%). There was also a social function of parent support groups, including the chance to meet other parents (91%) and children with disabilities (66%), the chance to meet others of similar culture and religion (69%) and language (59%), and the chance to have some kind of social life (63%).

While the information-giving and social functions of support groups were clearly valued by parents, we have already seen that parental awareness of services did not necessarily translate into additional service support. This, coupled with the lack of practical support received by parents to enable them to attend support groups, may be why parents rated them as not particularly helpful to them.

The few parents in the Phase 1 and Phase 3 interviews who did have access to support groups reported that they particularly valued the emotional support and advice received from other parents, which reduced parents' sense of isolation. It is worth noting that, for these parents, parent support groups were almost all run by and located within special schools.

There should be meetings for carers where you can get information and advice and meet other parents. It will make you feel less guilty as other parents will also ask for the same help. I feel isolated and I don't know how the other carers cope... I want a chance to talk to Asian mums and compare, in order to reassure myself and not feel guilty about using services.

Henna

I go to get reassurance that I am taking care of Erum well.

Hawra

When I go to the school they [other parents] tell me about their child and I tell them about my child. This helps by making my heart feel at peace, after seeing each other and meeting each other as friends. And the teachers also say come and visit the school and meet each other regularly. This way one feels a little happier.

Faiza

It is pointless telling them [extended family] anything because straight away they will say 'He'll get better'. Since I started going to the Asian support group at the school I have met both Asian and English mothers and you can talk to them and they will make you feel better by just listening. They have weekly meetings for the mothers at the school and some have two or more disabled children. I used to feel that I was the only one in this situation... That made me feel more patient.

Roshni

If I need some advice then I might phone [name of support group], the mothers and parents support group for children with disabilities and tell them what's happening and ask them 'What do you think?', you know? When I started going to this support group I started becoming a person again and thinking 'Yes, it's not just me. There's lots of us out there'. And knowing that my little gang is out there if I ever need them to talk to and just reassure me that I'm not on my own keeps me going you know... I mean I'd not see them for months and the other day I phoned and I said, 'Are you all there? Are you still there?' And they said 'Yes, we're still here don't worry about it and if you ever need us you know where we are. We haven't forgotten you'.

Shahina

Most parents in the Phase 1 and Phase 3 interviews preferred carers' groups to be ethnically mixed, although some parents did express a preference for ethnically specific carers' groups. Parents in favour of mixed groups saw a number of advantages for themselves and their child with disabilities, and saw themselves as having a lot in common with White parents.

> Mixed groups are better because we can talk and advise each other and the English mums know more about services.
>
> *Hawra*

> I prefer mixed groups, although I myself will only be able to speak to the Asian mums. English mothers are very friendly and also have more information than Asians.
>
> *Shaziza*

> You get a feel of everything and I was brought up in this country.
>
> *Firdaus*

> A mixed group is better as we should know their thoughts and feelings, as they will have had some similar experiences and know [more] than we do as they don't have a language problem. They [White English parents] are also more confident and this gives us confidence and makes us aware of our rights.
>
> *Roshni*

> Why should we separate ourselves? We should treat each other as equals with similar needs. We are not more special. It looks bad. It should be equal. They [White English parents] also have disabled children and I have also seen English mums very upset.
>
> *Zora*

> Mixed support groups are better as you should not narrow your children to just one ethnic group. You should broaden their horizons so that they don't become racist when they're older… You should not segregate your children and create Pakistan in the UK. This will just cause difficulties and we should learn to live with each other.
>
> *Shahina*

Parents preferring specific carers' groups also mentioned several advantages of this approach.

An Asian only group is better because we feel free to speak in our own language. If an English person was sat there then I would feel rude and ignorant speaking in my own language.

Amani

...because our needs are different. For example, we need to visit family in Pakistan for two months or so. So our problems are different.

Akhmal

Asians have a similar understanding, similar concerns and similar needs to talk about.

Sarah

We need a separate group as Asians have more difficulties due to the language barrier. I don't mind English mums coming however, it's just that Asian mums are left behind more.

Ayesha

Keyworkers

A keyworker is a service professional who helps families gain access to services and co-ordinates services for the family. Keyworkers have been shown in UK studies to address unmet parental needs and improve parental well-being among White families (Baldwin and Carlisle 1994; Beresford 1995). However, Chamba *et al.* (1999) reported that only one-third of families across different ethnic minority groups had a keyworker. In our study, even fewer Phase 2 families (28%) reported having a keyworker, although as in the Chamba *et al.* (1999) study most parents with a keyworker found them helpful (89% of parents with a keyworker). Most parents without a keyworker wanted one (59% of all parents), although a substantial minority (13%) felt that a keyworker could not help them. There were no differences across ethnic groups in the proportion of parents having a keyworker.

Although very few parents in the Phase 1 and Phase 3 interviews reported having a dedicated keyworker, some of them described how a health visitor or social worker had in effect taken on a keyworker role, informing parents of the available service support options and organising integrated support services. Some parents in the Phase 1 and Phase 3 interviews also reported that the person in the keyworker role had a crucial emotional support role, particularly in helping parents accept their child's disability.

It was OK [accessing service support] because when my health visitor [with interpreter] would visit she would arrange help for me. Basically everyone got together at the beginning to tell me that I can get such and such help.

Roshni

Well it was quite easy [accessing services] because my social worker did it all. So it was quite easy to know...what is available for children. You know for mothers who have got disabled children... Like when I needed help during my pregnancy I got a lot of help. Like my social worker gave me a lot of funding. And she got me a lot of help with [name of child with disabilities].

Amani

Well she [social worker] gradually explained things to me. She told me about Layla's care and asked me how I would take care of Layla... I never asked her for anything and all the work she did was from herself. She applied for Layla's expenses and arranged transport for all of Layla's appointments... She also told me that Layla will go to a special school... The social worker has shown me that there are supports available in this country and she went everywhere with me... The social worker took me there and I chose the school myself.

Huda

I was explained [by a South Asian social worker] about his feeding and his play. I was given a lot of information about his care. That he needs more support and attention... She [helped me to accept the disability] so I accepted this fact... Then she filled the forms for us and did everything needed.

Zareena

I would not agree to [financial support] at first and neither would my husband, as we felt that the cost of her [child with disabilities] care was our responsibility as God has given our daughter to us. Then [name of social worker] said 'Your child is entitled to financial help'. She then applied for disability benefits for us and day by day our expenditure increased. So I am glad of the financial support. It has made life easier for Layla as I am able to buy whatever she needs.

Huda

Nobody, no professional person ever, ever said to us 'Well you can get this help or that help or this'. Nobody, nobody. It was from the health visitor. She got in touch with services.

Nasreen

She was a social worker. She helped me everywhere... Whenever I phoned her if I needed anything she would make an appointment and come down, help my wife. Any sort of need I had she was always there... She helped me not only with the benefits moneywise but benefits like where Umber could stay overnight.

Arslan

He [social worker] helped us a lot for our son's sake. By writing and filling in forms he helped us out on many different aspects... He helped us a lot and showed us how to help ourselves.

Mariah

It is easier if it is an Asian woman, as I would feel more comfortable with a woman in my house. Also I would be able to discuss my daughter's personal problems fully.

Zora

The absence of a reliable, named individual to act as a point of contact inhibited access to service supports.

That's one of the other problems that the social services... We have no sort of set contact names or people they just come... Apparently [we have a social worker] but we don't know the name 'cos they keep changing and it's a big problem. We have to get to know each new person. Also if we need any help we don't know who to contact you see 'cos it's not exactly just one person. So contacting them can be a problem.

Akhmal

We didn't have any help at all... I think when you bring a small baby home and he's disabled and handicapped, I think there should be somebody there that has experienced talking to people and have met people. There's Asian people that have got nobody who can talk Asian or Punjabi, that can sit down to explain to them that there's other people in this situation that can make them hopeful...about the situation or about the facilities.

Firdaus

However, some parents in the Phase 3 interviews mentioned that a keyworker could be an indirect source of frustration for parents as the keyworker could raise parental expectations of services that were not delivered.

> When I have asked my keyworker for help she has done her best, but sometimes she tells me things that I can get and then when I ask her for certain things she says 'We'll do it' and then towards the end 'The Government won't give the money for it', which is very disappointing and frustrating. I always hear 'We don't have the money for this, we don't have the money for that'.
>
> *Zora*

> When I have not received help after being told about it I feel very frustrated and discriminated against.
>
> *Zakiya*

> I feel angry with my keyworker. Because I know the help is there, but because I'm not getting it, it's causing vibes and distress.
>
> *Shahina*

Services needed by families

In the Phase 1 and Phase 3 interviews, we asked parents in some depth about what services they needed, and whether or not these services actually existed. Parents in these interviews discussed a number of changes to services that would greatly improve their lives.

Drop-in centres

Most of the parents in the Phase 1 and Phase 3 interviews reported that a drop-in centre could significantly improve their lives. These centres would be available to be used by families in the evenings, at weekends and during family emergencies such as funerals. These centres would not require appointments or pre-booking, and would be geared to meeting the needs both of the child with disabilities and siblings.

> There should be a centre like apart from school in the evenings where you can take him [child with disabilities] to... Especially our Muslim people aren't doing enough to help Muslim people... Pakistani Muslims need a push.
>
> *Firdaus*

If there was some help in crisis situations so that if I need to go somewhere in an emergency. Respite is pre-booking, but if one needs to go suddenly to a funeral or something. If there was a place where they [two boys with disabilities] could be left.

Samaya

I wish there was some kind of group for, and it was run by Asian people for Asian parents... Not for people just to you know make fun of... If it was there for someone who really needed it, like when I have appointments 'cos sometimes I get these appointments [concerning the child with disabilities]... That drop-in centre for all the children. I think that would benefit a lot of people... I mean I end up sometimes going to the hospital and with the other children and because they're messing about and getting bored I end up, I can't ask the questions I want to ask. And in the long run...it's not me who suffers because I did not ask the question, it's Sayed because I've not been able to listen to what the doctors explained to me or I've not been able to ask any questions.

Nasreen

I just want that if I have a problem or any other reason and if they could look after Iman it will be really helpful. I don't mean when I'm at home. I mean when there's a death in the family then there is a big problem taking all of my children. There have been so many deaths in the family and I couldn't go because there was no one to look after my children.

Azra

Well it's mostly weekends are very bad then weekdays, because he's at home like full stop. And sometimes it just gets too much... My family is not happy [about using respite services] and neither would I settle overnight you see... Because he's never been away from home, I don't think he'll settle. [What would make life easier would be] if it was like during the day thing. If maybe he goes somewhere during the day and comes back in the evening, like you know he goes to school and he comes back. If they had something like that, not overnight.

Amani

Parents generally preferred their child with disabilities to be in groups appropriate to their skills and behaviours.

This [centre] is also necessary in the evenings as Parveen cries when she comes home, as I am not able to provide the attention that she needs, due to my home responsibilities and my other children.

Ayesha

It would be better than respite care, as a daytime service doesn't cause as much guilt.

Henna

Those who cannot defend themselves should be separate from those who can run around and have behaviour problems. I have seen an incident where a more able child forced his hand into the mouth of a more severely disabled child causing distress and pain to the child.

Akhmal

My child is able to walk around and mix with children. I would want him with those children who can also run around and play with him. I would also want supervision at all times as he does hit others badly and he may be hit by others.

Zakiya

Parents also generally expressed the view that drop-in centres should be for people from all ethnic groups rather than specialist centres being set up for families from specific ethnic communities.

Because it is very important to get to know other people too, as we live and have to adapt to the different cultures. Haider would also feel more comfortable when meeting other people outside.

Akram

They are mixed at the school and it is wrong to ask for a separate service. We cannot ask to be separate and then ask for help from them [non-Asians] at the same time... It is the quality of care that matters.

Zora

It should be for any child really. We have to adapt to English ways as we live in this country. English children are still humans and they still have the same problems. The only downfall really is the language barrier.

Shahina

The emphasis for the parents was on fun activities for the child, with staff experienced in working with disabled children from a range of communities.

> The activities should be sort of physiotherapy type, aromatherapy type and whirlpool activities. The activities should stop the children from getting bored and sensory rooms would be nice and pleasant for the children... They should have staff experienced with disabled children and who have been actively involved.
>
> *Firdaus*

> Activities should be fun, music, TV, dance.
>
> *Henna*

> They should have entertaining play activities to distract the child and keep the child happy, to settle a child.
>
> *Azra*

> It should be sporty, physical activities, football, painting, going for walks, swimming, pictures, etc.
>
> *Shahina*

Support at home

Many parents described needing practical support with housework and helping with supervising or nursing the child with disabilities. Parents also mentioned wanting advice on managing difficult child behaviour. Effective home support would help the whole family, by helping the child with disabilities to develop skills and have a more active life, and by giving parents and siblings a break. As has been mentioned elsewhere in this chapter, satisfactory support at home was rarely offered by services and, where it was offered, it was often seen as actively unhelpful and not taken up for long.

> Someone should come in and help with housework or supervising the child. It will give parents a break from the mental and physical stress of the 24-hour care of an ill child.
>
> *Firdaus*

> There should be more practical help like ironing and hoovering to take the burden off the mum and allow her to rest after night care. I had this assistance and even after a 15-minute break I had rested and benefited.
>
> *Ayesha*

I have three disabled boys… When they were sick I was always feeding, changing nappies, changing bedding, etc. It was the most difficult time. The health service nurses should help in the house or with the child…it gives reassurance to parents about the well-being of their child and parents get a break.

Zareena

Parents need teaching on how to manage behaviour when their child is not well behaved.

Duaa

If your child has behaviour problems you need someone to advise and explain things.

Henna

Some parents also mentioned needing workers to come to spend time with the child with disabilities either inside or outside the house, to stimulate the child and give parents and siblings a break.

You should have access to a support worker at times of need when the child is too demanding for a few hours, in order to take the child out and entertain the child. So this service needs to be flexible.

Roshni

I need someone to come into the home and give him the one to one attention that he needs. It gives us a break and keeps spirits high that someone is out there for you.

Shahina

We need more support, sit-in carers who come in and take the pressure away from the brothers and sisters by giving the support to mum when it's needed.

Firdaus

I need someone to supervise Tahir in the evenings so that my children can do their homework and I can do my house chores.

Zakiya

Gender-specific services

Many parents in the Phase 1 and Phase 3 interviews wanted same-sex workers for their child with disabilities, particularly for personal care tasks, and some parents wanted separate services for older boys and girls.

> If I had a daughter then I would be concerned about male carers. I would be more wary if I had a daughter. Asians therefore need more female carers.
>
> *Firdaus*

> We do need female carers for changing the nappy of a female child.
>
> *Zora*

> I think the needs are different for females. If I had a female child then I would feel more comfortable talking to a professional female than a male.
>
> *Amani*

> We just need a separate female service in night services, respite services. There is not such a problem with mixing during the day, as long as the children are supervised.
>
> *Shaziza*

> With male children it is easier to use outside services such as respite, but for a female child we need female carers which makes it more difficult to use services.
>
> *Akhmal*

Ethnically integrated services

Parents in the Phase 3 interviews were asked in some detail about whether they would prefer separate services based on ethnicity, or mixed-ethnicity services. In general, all parents interviewed preferred services to be integrated across ethnic groups, but with services routinely meeting their cultural and religious needs. There were two main reasons for this general preference: the need for different communities to mix, and the commonality of interests of disabled families across ethnic groups.

> It is very important to get to know other people too…adapt to the different cultures. Haider would also feel comfortable meeting others outside.
>
> *Akram*

Mixed services with English and Asian children are best because children need to learn about society.

Duaa

I don't want separate Asian services. It is not right as you will be isolating yourself from this community and this culture...it will make you feel uncomfortable approaching other mixed services.

Henna

I don't think it will be right because we should be more involved with the different communities. We should not try to separate ourselves from these English, West Indian and other communities, especially as the needs are common with the other communities as well. So why be separate? When it comes to religious needs they are respected, so why be separate?

Jabir

There should just be services where language support is provided. This is more important than separate services as it's the communication that is essential.

Azra

Mixed services are better as English staff could be trained to understand Asian needs.

Zakiya

Staff skills and staff training

As we have seen, parents generally reported wanting integrated services across ethnic communities, as long as the language, cultural and religious needs of families were met. Parents in the Phase 3 interviews suggested two major ways that staff in integrated services could be helped to meet the needs of South Asian families. The first was to appoint more South Asian staff throughout mainstream services.

I think the social services should provide language support by employing Asian support workers depending on the ratio of people in ethnic minorities who are disabled. There are a very small number of Asian support workers.

Jabir

There should be more Asian keyworkers as families need one to one support at times.

Ayesha

They don't always provide interpreters at the hospitals and there should be more Asian staff. This would benefit us due to the greater cultural and religious understanding and language support.

Azra

Second, parents also mentioned ways that White staff in services could be trained to meet their language, cultural and religious needs.

They need to know about our food and different culture. These issues should be taught within each professional nursing or medical course.

Akhmal

Non-Asian staff should have the motivation to learn about all the different cultures and religions... I have had contact with non-Asian staff who have picked up the needs of Asians well and tried very much to meet them.

Shaziza

You can teach them the practical aspects of religion like halal food and festive occasions. They could also be taken to Asian shops, mosques and take-aways to 'feel' some of the culture.

Akram

A lot of people already know a lot, for example, that we're fasting or that Eid is coming soon. For example, my neighbour was so interested in our religion and she was so keen on Asian food. We need a laid-back approach to teach professionals.

Amani

We should answer all their questions and fears and tell them the basics.

Ayesha

Teachers should also know the Asian languages a little to communicate with children who don't understand English.

Sarah

Unmet needs

Previous research with UK families across a range of ethnic groups has reported substantial levels of unmet needs reported by parents of a child with severe learning disabilities (Beresford 1995; Chamba *et al.* 1999). As part of Phase 2 of our study we asked parents about 31 different family needs and whether they were met, using questions from Chamba *et al.* (1999). Table 6.3 lists these family needs and the percentage of parents who rated each need as unmet. Overall, the parents in our study reported much higher levels of unmet needs than previous UK research, including research with South Asian parents of a child with severe disabilities (Beresford 1995; Chamba *et al.* 1999). Consistent with other findings throughout our study, unmet information needs had a high priority for parents, along with unmet needs concerning care for the child outside school to give carers a break, an unmet need for holidays with the child and unmet financial needs. Most parents also reported they needed help in planning for the child's future.

Similarly to the Chamba *et al.* study, there were a number of differences in unmet needs across ethnic groups, with Bangladeshi parents reporting fewer unmet needs than Indian or Pakistani parents in seven areas. However, in the areas of emergency health care and emergency child care Pakistani parents reported higher levels of unmet need than Indian or Bangladeshi parents.

The future

Evidence from the 1991 Census suggested that South Asian young adults with learning disabilities were half as likely to be living in residential services compared to their White counterparts (Emerson and Hatton 1998). However, very little research has investigated the opinions of South Asian parents of children with disabilities concerning future service options for their child. In our study we asked parents about whether they had any plans for the child's future, how those plans had been arrived at and what those plans were.

Only 23 per cent of parents in the Phase 2 interviews reported that they had plans for the future of their child with disabilities, with parents of older children slightly more likely to have plans. Where parents had discussed future plans for the child, this had tended to occur within the immediate family (23% of all parents) rather than with extended family members (3.7%) or professionals (5.9%).

Parents were also asked if they had considered a range of options for the future care of their child. Most parents preferred future care to continue to be provided by the family (78%), with Bangladeshi parents more likely to prefer

Table 6.3 Unmet needs of parents across ethnic groups: Phase 2			
Unmet need for parent	**Indian (%)**	**Pakistani (%)**	**Bangladeshi (%)**	**All Parents (%)**
---	---	---	---	---
Shown services available	96	90	73	90
Help to explore education options	91	86	60	84
Learn best way to help child	91	85	53	83
Help in school holidays	86	82	73	81
Help planning child's future	82	85	47	81
Break from caring for child	86	77	73	79
Support in relevant language	68	81	87	79
Help to travel/go on holiday with child	91	80	60	79
More money to care for child	73	77	79	77
Contact with South Asian staff	59	74	73	71
Help to do things parent enjoys	73	75	47	71
Someone to talk to	73	72	47	70
Emergency health care	59	78	33	70
Emergency child care	55	79	33	69
Help spending time with other children	82	69	20	65
Help with community/family events	64	67	47	64
Help finding future care	73	61	60	63
Help with child problem behaviour	73	63	33	62
More furniture/clothes/toys	64	57	53	58
Expand parents' own education	68	57	33	57
Help with day to day care of child	50	64	33	59
Adaptations of the house for child	64	56	27	54
Spend more time with spouse	59	52	13	50
Help getting the child to sleep better	50	47	40	47
Help with housework	59	46	27	46
Meet other parents of disabled children	50	47	33	46

Help with transport	59	41	53	46
Help getting respite care	41	44	27	42
Help getting a preferred school place	55	27	0	30
Help feeding child	36	28	13	28
Having a child minder so parent. can work	36	21	7	22

this option. A further 22 per cent of parents reported considering a residential placement option for their child, with Indian parents more likely to prefer this option. Only 2.2 per cent of parents reported an arranged marriage as a possible future option for their child. However, it is worth noting that over half of parents (56%) were not sure in their preference for any future care option.

Parents in the Phase 1 and Phase 3 interviews whose children with severe learning disabilities were reaching school leaving age expressed considerable concern about the future. Some parents did not know what, if any, post-education services were available. Other parents had discussed post-education services with professionals from adult services, but expressed concerns about their quantity and cultural appropriateness, sometimes leading to the refusal of services offered.

It doesn't seem to me that anything else would help me more than this help [school and benefits]... I'm worried about Bilal because he's older now, his school ends next year. He's going to school now and I don't have no worries...after 19 his school will finish. If there is no job or anything like that for him then he'll stay at home...he won't be able to work... I do get a little worried when I think what will happen next. Because they say that they've opened up such services but I'll have to drop him off and bring him back myself. Maybe when he's 19 life will change and become a little difficult... I won't have what I have now where the school takes him from nine o'clock in the morning till three o'clock.

Zareena

She's [child with disabilities] older now. Now what will they do for her in the future?... What will I do now? I don't understand that much about her. Nor am I educated that I could go somewhere else...that's why I was asking you that now that she's 16 what do I do? Do you have to take her [child with disabilities] to sign on or will she have a book or what? That is what I don't know.

Hawra

I had so many forms when Humaria was 16 and Humaria cannot complete them. I cannot read and I don't know the language. This has caused considerable distress as I do not have access to Asian staff to complete the many forms for me.

Shaziza

He's going to school, what's going to happen when he gets to 16? What facilities are gonna be available then?

Firdaus

Our biggest worry is his future. We do not consider him a burden but we worry about what will happen in the future.

Duaa

I have many questions about what will happen after school at college etc. Will she just go for three days? We need full-time support at that time too. I cannot do anything when she is at home. Parents need early information and reassurance.

Ayesha

I hope that once he [child with disabilities] leaves school there's still a lot more going on for him because I believe that after 18 there isn't a hell of a lot more for these children. What I'm gonna do with him is a worry in itself. I think with support they should carry on with colleges for them and people should be a little more considerate depending on his ability perhaps with a little part-time job. 'Cos there's a lot of ignorance towards these children.

Shahina

One time I've been asked by [name of special school], because my daughter is going to an adult service, 'Do I mind if her nappy is changed by a male rather than a female'... Sometimes they have to because sometimes they haven't got female staff so they have to be male, and bathing and things like that. This is where I feel it's not fair or right so I say that and they say they will look into it to get a better female service... We've been asked what [religion] we are, then you get Muslim food and things like that. I think everything should be like that.

Arslan

They asked me about college for her [child with disabilities] and I didn't accept. I said that if a child is mentally alert then he can take care of himself, but Humaria is not like that and if they are all females then I give you my permission. They said there are also boys. So I didn't accept.

Shaziza

A keyworker could be invaluable in the transition from education services to services for adults.

It was hard when he was leaving school. We did not know how to ask for information ourselves. The school arranged a worker who helped us a lot by taking us to a lot of day centres. She helped us to decide which place was best for fulfilling Ali's needs. She came every week and also helped with his welfare benefits. We did not have any major problems.

Akram

Beyond school, most parents in the Phase 1 and Phase 3 interviews wanted adult day services to continue to educate and stimulate the child. For parents whose children were currently experiencing adult day centre services, there was a stark contrast between what they wanted and what their child was experiencing.

There should be a support group. They could take Bilal to places where he can do some activities that he enjoys, a facility where they are entertained with activities or taken out.

Zareena

After school they should go to college and I would like him to go as often as he can cope with.

Amani

There should be some sort of a regular centre where they can go along during the day. It should be active, not just for people to sit down and watch telly and such. There should be properly trained staff and teachers who do things with them. There should also be a nurse available. It is not enough just to have carers there. The children need to be active and stimulated.

Firdaus

Education should continue for their ability level in schools. I don't think a normal day centre is appropriate. After school finishes it's like life ends for these children and you have to take them out and do everything for them.

Henna

The college is better. They should perhaps change the day centre environment to a college environment, as the child could then continue education according to his/her ability level and become a little independent.

Roshni

Parents in the Phase 1 interviews also reported concern about what would happen to their child if they became too ill to care for the child or died.

The only thing that keeps on worrying me about him [child with disabilities] is that what is going to happen tomorrow, if me and my wife, if we die tomorrow. That's something which keeps on worrying me about his future care. I'm not worried about the next ten years. I'll put up with what I can. It's only what's going to happen tomorrow…if we're not around… So far I've got nothing planned. I'm always very optimistic that my children will look after him but it depends.

Jabir

All parents worry about their children, about their education, about growing up, about their subsequent marriage and their families, but these kind of children need constant support. They do not grow up like normal children in the sense that they cannot have their own families or somebody to look after them in the future… What will happen to him after us, as he needs support all his life? As he grows older we constantly think about what will he do in life. His brothers love him and they reassure me that they will look after him, but we do not know about time.

Duaa

Very few parents in the Phase 1 and Phase 3 interviews had discussed long-term plans for their child with disabilities, with three parents considering the possibility of an arranged marriage for their child and one parent considering residential care. Only a few parents felt they could rely on family members for the future care of their child.

I would prefer him to stay with the family. If the family did not support him I would like him to stay in a caring centre with a caring environment, such as that at school. They should have a similar environment as the home, with halal food, meat and other religious needs.

Zareena

We prefer a special care centre for mixed Asians and non-Asians, but female carers for girls.

Azra

If I was no longer around I would need help for Faizal. I would need a good place for him to live. It should be like home and similar to the way he has been brought up at home. It should be an Asian place for Asians only. However, I would prefer the staff to be mixed because Asians are not as thorough as English staff.

Duaa

Well in five or ten years time we are thinking if he [child with disabilities] is in a condition to look after himself... So we are thinking if he's a bit better I mean you know look after himself, or if he is able just to make arrangements for his marriage in our people you know, in relations. So we will be happy because they will look after him... In that way we will be able to get someone to look after him. I mean you know his wife.

Akram

A loving, caring, Muslim, Asian family would be more appropriate and familiar for Amir. In a centre different people come and go, which is more unstable for the child. He needs a consistent relationship with somebody who learns to understand him.

Firdaus

I've actually thought about that [residential care] and I think it depends on my home circumstances and how Yusuf develops because obviously if it gets to a stage where he's still too much for me to cope and he's getting bigger and bigger and a grown man, then basically I'm gonna have to think about that seriously when the time comes.

Shahina

I asked my eldest daughter-in-law one day that if anything should happen to me would she be able to care for Parveen. She assured me that I need not worry about that. She will look after Parveen... She needs a good understanding environment.

Ayesha

I would like Layla to stay with my daughter-in-law, but with support from outside.

Huda

Parents' dreams about the future for their child varied depending on the optimism of the parent. Parents with less optimism about their child reported dreams that their child was normal, which were contrasted with the bleak reality that parents felt.

We want him [child with disabilities] to have a good education, have a good job, spend his life like our other children so that he does not have to depend on anybody.

Duaa

That she [child with disabilities] has a good education. She gets married and has her own house and family. This is my wish.

Ayesha

When I look at her [child with disabilities] I can only see darkness. I would like that if there was a less disabled boy in Nadia's school so that she could get married to him. Nadia should be taken for what she is.

Henna

I do not have any dreams for his [child with disabilities] future... If Allah could release him from such misery I would be happy for him, because he suffers a lot.

Mariah

My dreams would be for him [child with disabilities] to get better and for him to study etc. like normal children. It would also be for him to marry, but he can't do anything. I don't have any dreams as they won't be fulfilled.

Faiza

Other parents with more optimism tended to report more realistic dreams for the future, in terms of improvements in the child's skills and health and increased independence.

[My dream is] that we mother and child live together [laughs]. There are dreams that my child be normal, come back with some degree then get married, but for [name of child with disabilities] my dream is just that he becomes independent and starts taking care of himself, just a little for himself. For me just this would be something for me to feel happy about. He's 17 and he still needs to be dressed and everything. If he becomes independent then there is nothing else that would make me happier.

Zareena

Just that she [child with disabilities] will be able to walk properly by herself and go here and there. She can't go here and there now unless there is someone with her, and she walks like normal children do but she doesn't walk properly. If she walks by herself she looks as though she's going to fall...she wears the pads on her knees.

Hawra

Really I would like him [child with disabilities] to be able to talk and if he couldn't talk, even if he could use sign language, just sign, just make himself noticed.

Nasreen

Hopefully, I hope that he [child with disabilities] has a place of his own one day and he's independent you know [laughs]. My life might start at 40 [laughs].

Shahina

I think that their life [two children with disabilities] will be more comfortable if they had the things they need, for example better property and other things as mentioned earlier.

Samaya

I want to take her [child with disabilities] and you know like she's happy if there's you know a big garden. A park and stuff. She likes a big place to run about in and everything and I want to take her to Pakistan for a holiday.

Sarah

The relationship between formal and informal support

In the Phase 1 and Phase 3 interviews, it was obvious that parental experiences of informal and formal service supports were not independent. Informal and formal supports, or the lack of them, clearly influenced each other. A small minority of parents in these interviews described what they considered to be the most supportive relationship, where both informal and formal supports were available and complemented each other.

> I don't even find out any help because they [services] ask me 'Do you need any help?'... Everything is OK [laughs]... The benefits lady came to see me, she said herself that she'd send me a form... My sister-in-law helped me to fill the form, she's very helpful about these things. So I found it easy... I ask her advice first about what I should do. She phones the agencies or the school to ask what we have to do...and she will explain to me... She finds out everything for me.
>
> *Zareena*

> It was when Irfan was seriously ill. There was a problem in going to see him at the hospital regularly... Then I had a word with my social worker about the young one [second child with disabilities] and the difficulty in going to the hospital. My friend used to help me at times. The social worker said she will arrange for my friend to be paid to do this work permanently. So she gets paid now.
>
> *Samaya*

As described in Chapter 4, for several parents a lack of formal support in terms of appropriate diagnosis had hindered parental understanding and acceptance of their child's disability. This had resulted in parents finding it difficult to mobilise support from family, friends or support services.

> It's like we were kept in the dark for four years. We did not know anything... We treated her as a normal child. We did not feel any of her special needs. Other children considered her as 'dumb', mentally not well and that she is not intelligent. It might have helped if there was information in Asian...nobody thought [the child's disability] was a big issue, even her father. Only I felt there was something wrong... Nobody understood... We never thought that this would be forever. We thought she will be cured.
>
> *Henna*

He [husband] will just say 'I don't feel like going [to the appointment] and what can the doctor do? He's not going to make Harron better'. I just say that he is not going to get better sitting at home either. Whenever Harron has to have a test of any sort he [husband] will say 'What is the point of making Harron suffer?' Now I don't ask him. I just go ahead and have it done.

Roshni

The most common relationship between informal and formal support described by parents in the Phase 1 interviews was the use of formal support to compensate for the absence of informal support, particularly from extended family and friends. This resulted in parents not only requiring practical support from services, but also emotional support.

My son and daughter-in-law are going to Pakistan in two months for a short while... Then I will ask [social worker] for the home help so that I will not be alone in taking care of Layla... I have never asked family for help because my immediate family is in Pakistan. I have two nieces here but they are married into someone else's family and have their own responsibilities. They cannot come and help without the permission of their families... I am happy [with the help from the social worker]... She will do what she can for me.

Huda

At the moment we have the Crossroads care assistant who comes every morning. And then [name of support worker] comes and she helps me with the housework... At the minute my family you know they take Shaukhat for an afternoon or something like that, but at the minute my mum's been through an operation and that. So I don't get much help from them. And plus you can't rely on your family all the time. You need, you know you have to get into a routine where you know that you can cope and you have to do it yourself. And use help which is available.

Amani

I would say like we were very worried about his school holidays and I was thinking that we will let Sharukh go to the relatives during the daytime and spend some of the time there. So that he will get fresh and we'll have a bit of a break, but...it's better if he's looked after by social services, because if he's got any problems when he's with relatives they won't know what to do if they can't find us. But the social services will know what to do. So they're arranging respite now.

Jabir

You can say that they [friends and family] were sympathetic, but no one understood. My sister had some idea of how upsetting it was for me, even she did not think that the problem was too great... It is enough that someone [from outside] comes and talks and listens to what I am suffering. So that I can talk to them in my own language... Because our families try to hide from the outside world that there is any problem in the family.

Henna

Summary

The findings of our study regarding semi-formal and formal service supports are in some respects similar to previous UK research with minority ethnic families with a person with disabilities (Chamba *et al*. 1999; Hatton *et al*. 1998). However, the parents in our study report lower levels of service awareness and receipt and higher levels of unmet needs than previous UK research.

As with previous research (Hatton *et al.* 1998), parents generally reported high awareness of general health and welfare services and also high awareness of education and allied services. Indian parents and parents using the English language were more likely to be aware of services. Family uptake of services, with the exception of GP and school services, was much lower. Indian parents and English language users were again more likely to receive some services although differences were fewer and less dramatic than differences in awareness, possibly due to the generally low levels of service uptake. Schools were consistently rated by parents as the most helpful services, although parental views of the helpfulness of GPs and social workers were very mixed. A helpful GP or social worker was viewed as invaluable and as facilitating access to service supports, but an unhelpful one could be damaging and a hindrance to service awareness and uptake.

Just under half of parents in the Phase 2 interviews (43%) reported a collaborative relationship with service professionals. Problems with services experienced by most parents included communication and information barriers, and the long delays and constant fighting to gain service support. Bangladeshi parents reported fewer problems with services in a number of areas, possibly due to lower expectations of services. Indian parents reported more problems communicating with services and services understanding less about their culture. English language use was also associated with having to fight less to get service support. Parents in the Phase 1 interviews reported that fights to get service support could last several years, leading to great parental frustration and a lack of confidence in professionals.

Almost all the children with disabilities in the study were in special schools, which were generally very highly rated by parents. Parents reported that special schools were good for the child, good for them as parents because they gave them a break, and often the only reliable point of contact with services to gain information and support. Schools were also generally reported as responsive to parental concerns about the child. However, very few schools provided for the cultural or religious needs of the children, and parents were also concerned about the availability and quality of speech therapy and physiotherapy and the lack of any teaching in the relevant Asian language for the child. All these areas were priorities for improvement according to parents. A small minority of Phase 1 parents reported dissatisfaction with special schools in terms of poor standards of care and a lack of parental choice.

Few parents reported awareness and uptake of short-term care/respite care services for their child, although upon being made aware of respite care services during the research interviews almost half of parents (42%) reported wanting respite care services. Almost all respite care received was in respite units managed by social services; these services were generally highly valued and sometimes responsive to the child's cultural needs, but insufficient for parental needs. Problems with respite services cited by some parents included long waiting lists, not being able to use respite services at short notice, and a lack of confidence in the ability of respite care professionals to care for the child.

Among parents who were aware of but had not used respite care services, the most common reasons for not using respite services were the child not liking to stay away overnight, the risk of their child being abused, and services providing culturally inappropriate care. Parental ideas to improve respite care services included raising parental awareness, raising the cultural awareness of respite services, making respite services easily accessible, having staff who know the child well and having same-sex respite carers.

Although 65 per cent of parents in the Phase 2 interviews reported needing an interpreter, only 40 per cent of parents had been provided with one. Where used, interpreters were highly valued, with parents particularly appreciating being able to say what they wanted confidentially without having to rely on family or friends for interpretation. Parents who had not used an interpreter reported most commonly relying on their partner or another child in the family for help with interpreting.

A minority of parents reported being aware of or participating in family support groups. Parents valued the information they obtained at these groups, and the chance to meet other parents and gain emotional support. However, the helpfulness of these groups to parents was limited, possibly because attendance did not result in increased service support.

A minority of parents (28%) reported having a keyworker, with social workers and health visitors often taking on a keyworker role. Where provided, keyworkers were almost always viewed as invaluable, in terms of raising parental awareness of benefits and services, organising integrated service supports, and providing ongoing emotional support.

Parents in the Phase 1 and Phase 3 interviews particularly mentioned drop-in centres, effective home support services and gender-specific services as having the potential to greatly improve family life. Parents in the Phase 3 interviews also expressed a preference for ethnically integrated services that routinely met their child's language, cultural and religious needs.

Given the general lack of awareness and service support reported by parents, it was unsurprising that the range of unmet needs reported by parents was extremely high, substantially higher than reported in comparable UK research (Chamba *et al.* 1999). A vast majority of Phase 2 parents reported unmet needs in terms of a lack of information, a lack of support outside school time and during school holidays, insufficient finance and a need for help with planning the child's future. Bangladeshi parents reported lower unmet needs in a range of areas, although Pakistani parents reported greater unmet needs in emergency health and child care.

Parents reported a general lack of certainty about future plans for their child with disabilities. Less than a quarter of parents in the Phase 2 interviews (23%) had discussed future plans, usually within the immediate family. The major expressed preference of parents was for their child to continue living with the family with support. Residential care was a less considered option, although most parents were not certain about their preferred option. Parents with a child about to leave school reported considerable uncertainty and confusion about the post-education service supports available. Those parents who had been in contact with adult services reported concerns about the cultural and religious appropriateness of the adult services offered.

Finally, for most parents in the Phase 1 interviews, formal support services were needed to compensate for a lack of informal supports. Very few parents reported complementary or collaborative relationships between informal and formal supports, with some parents consequently reporting a lack of emotional support from any source.

Chapter Seven

Family Social Life

Many previous studies have shown that families with a person with disabilities experience considerable restrictions on the social activities of both parents and children, with families from minority ethnic communities reporting greater restrictions than White families (Beresford 1995; Chamba *et al.* 1999; Hatton *et al.* 1998; Sloper *et al.* 1990). In our study, the social life of the child and family was investigated with parents in the Phase 2 interviews using the Social Life Index, developed in a UK study of 123 families with a child with Down's syndrome (Sloper *et al.* 1990). In this section of the interview we asked about:

1. Parent social life and interests (time child can be left unsupervised, restrictions on parent social activities).

2. Child social life – organisation: an index based on the range and frequency of the child's involvement in organised activities (for example special needs social club, mosque).

3. Child social life – friends: an index based on the range and frequency of the child's involvement in social activities with friends (both with and without disabilities).

The social life of parents

For parents, the fact that their children required considerable supervision imposed considerable restrictions on their social lives. Almost half the parents in the Phase 2 interviews (43%) reported that their child could not be left unsupervised for even a moment, with a further 41 per cent reporting that their child could not be left unsupervised for more than an hour. Unsurprisingly, most parents (69%) thought this was a definite problem, with only 11 per cent reporting that the need to supervise their child was not a problem. Although there were no differences between ethnic groups in the length of time parents could leave their child unsupervised, Pakistani parents reported that the need to supervise their child was a greater problem than Indian or Bangladeshi parents.

Many parents in the Phase 2 interviews reported that caring for the child imposed wide-ranging restrictions on their social lives. Only 31 per cent of parents reported that they could at least sometimes go out in the evening, and only 25 per cent reported that they could at least sometimes go away for the weekend. Pakistani parents were less likely to go out in the evenings and away for the weekend than Indian and Bangladeshi parents.

The vast majority of parents (85% to 90%) reported that caring for their child resulted in social and leisure activities such as social outings, visits to friends, holidays, home leisure activities and hobbies being either restricted or completely cut out. Almost half of parents reported that they had completely cut out holidays. The only difference between ethnic groups was that Bangladeshi parents reported that caring for their child resulted in fewer restrictions on their home leisure activities than Indian and Pakistani parents.

Parents in the Phase 1 interviews also reported restrictions on their social lives, both in their day-to-day social lives and in plans to visit extended family in India, Pakistan or Bangladesh. These restrictions were increased if the child was in a single parent family and reduced if informal and/or formal support was available.

> No one helps me. I have not seen my mother for 14 years but I can't go to Pakistan because there is no one to look after my children in my absence and I can't take them with me because they do not have the same medicines or facilities as in England. The [name of hospital] said that they will keep Mumtaz for two weeks only but they had no space for Imtiaz. So I had to cancel my tickets.
>
> *Zora*

> It is very difficult now. My parents and brother and sisters are all in Pakistan. They ask me to come and see them. I cannot take Daniel with me... [I last went to Pakistan] about six or seven years ago.
>
> *Seema*

> Well our personal life has been spoilt because me and my wife couldn't go anywhere. Wherever we go I feel because there is no other member of our

family like that [with disabilities]. I think if I take Umber somewhere and she grabs things...so we have to leave her in a separate room. Plus Umber's got problems with walking; taking her upstairs and downstairs is hard work. People haven't got separate rooms in this country, so that way we don't go to parties, we don't go to weddings. If we wanted to go out with the full family somewhere we couldn't because it's not an easy life... At least one or two people need to support Umber.

Arslan

I haven't got any life. Most of my friends will visit here, because if we go there then basically you know it's actually babysitting Yusuf because you've got to keep an eye on him... He'll be bullying other kids or being silly with them... So at the end of the day I just end up getting them [friends] to come round. And I don't go out most evenings... I basically do nothing but work and come home, see to these [children], and do a bit of reading before I go to bed or I might watch a film on telly and that is my typical week after week routine. For a Saturday the house has to be cleaned upside-down and these have got to be ready for school.

Shahina [single parent]

After his [child with disabilities] illness was diagnosed it has affected us in such a manner that we cannot leave him and visit Bangladesh and we cannot leave him and go anywhere else. If we go anywhere we have to come back quickly. Somebody has to be with him all the time. Somebody has to do things for him. It is very traumatic for us.

Mariah

We are not affected by his disability that much... Even if we have to go somewhere we leave him with his aunt, but we do not leave him on his own.

Duaa

The social life of the child

The Social Life Index (Sloper *et al.* 1990) asked parents in the Phase 2 interviews for information about the range and frequency of the child's social activities in organisations and with friends. In both areas children can score from zero (no social activities) to 48 (maximum range and frequency of social contacts). For children of the parents in the Phase 2 interviews, 81 per cent of children scored zero on the organisations index, indicating no involvement in organised activities, a much higher figure than the 43 per cent of mainly

White children with Down's syndrome reported by Sloper *et al.* (1990). Similarly, 73 per cent of Phase 2 children scored zero on the friends index, indicating no involvement in social activities with friends, compared to 13 per cent of children with Down's syndrome (Sloper *et al.* 1990).

Sloper *et al.* (1990) also produced a total social life index, which adds the organisation and friends areas and also includes social contacts with siblings and same-age relatives (range 0–128). Here, 27 per cent of children scored zero, indicating no social activities with organisations, friends or siblings/same-age relatives, compared to none of the children with Down's syndrome (Sloper *et al.* 1990).

Indian children were more likely than Pakistani and Bangladeshi children to have some involvement in organised activities, and Bangladeshi children were less likely to be involved in any kind of social activity than Indian or Pakistani children.

These findings starkly illustrate the restrictions on social activities of children with severe learning disabilities from South Asian communities, and the reliance of children with disabilities on siblings for social contacts. Unsurprisingly, most parents (62%) were unhappy with their child's social life, with parents most often requesting evening and weekend activities for their child.

Parents in the Phase 1 interviews also reported substantial restrictions on the social lives and leisure activities of their child with disabilities. In the absence of formal service support, the social life of the child with disabilities was very dependent on parents. Restrictions on the child's social life were increased by negative attitudes from extended family and the general public, often resulting in leisure activities taking place largely in the home.

> We'll go out in the park, erm go to [name of shopping centre] and we'll go to my mum's. We'll go out and about shopping, visiting relatives and friends. Now weddings and funerals are a bit different…it can get a bit too much for Amir.
>
> *Firdaus*

> She really enjoys cooking at school. She also makes tea at home or sandwiches. She can't make anything else. She will make chips, beans, eggs and things like that.
>
> *Shaziza*

> In our family [parent lives with spouse's parents] no one understands that I need a break. I wish I could take Nadia out whenever she wants… I do but only when I have the mental strength and courage to speak up. She

likes to go into town or see a film. We went to a concert a few days ago. She has also been to Blackpool. She likes disco and dance. This is not seen as good in our family. She plays the music in the room sometimes but no one likes that.

Henna

He likes the tape. The music. I don't take him out. We have needed a bigger wheelchair for the last two to three years. I also don't take him out because people stare. He has become very thin now. When he was young I took him out. He looked just like a baby. He used to look normal then but now he's bigger and very thin... I do feel happy when they take him out to school.

Faiza

I enjoy playing football with him [child with disabilities] when the weather's nice. I enjoy toy fighting with him... I enjoy being silly with him [laughs]. I enjoy swimming with him. I enjoy playing hide-and-seek with him and I enjoy playing catch me games with him or reading with him.

Shahina

Summary

Parents reported considerable restrictions in both their social lives and those of their child with disabilities. Parents reported wide-ranging restrictions on their social and leisure activities, including nights out and weekends away, restrictions reported by a greater number of Pakistani families. These restrictions were made worse if the child needed constant supervision and if the family was headed by a single parent. Reliable informal and formal supports outside school hours helped parents have an active social life.

The social life of the child with disabilities was similarly restricted, with the vast majority of children having no social involvement with friends or organised activities. Unsurprisingly, most parents were unhappy with their child's social life, which was particularly restricted if the extended family and the general public were felt to hold negative attitudes towards the child with disabilities.

Chapter Eight

Parental Health

Although most UK research with parents of children with disabilities from ethnic minority communities has focused on service issues, some research has investigated the physical and mental health of parents (Hatton *et al.* 1998). Hatton *et al.* reported distress indicative of a mental health problem among 78 per cent of South Asian parents of a person with learning disabilities. This figure is much higher than other UK research using the same interview schedule with mainly White families (Kiernan and Alborz 1994; Sloper *et al.* 1988; Sloper and Turner 1991, 1994). Hatton *et al.* (1998) also found that parents reported a very high use of health services on their own behalf, suggesting high levels of physical health problems.

To explore the physical and mental health of parents in the Phase 2 interviews, our study used standardised, translated interview schedules from the Policy Studies Institute 4th National Survey (Nazroo 1997, 1998) of the UK population from minority ethnic communities. This allowed us to compare the parents in our study to large numbers of UK South Asian parents. The coping strategies used by South Asian parents were also investigated for the first time in our study. The health, well-being and coping strategies of parents were also discussed extensively in the Phase 1 interviews.

Parental coping

Parents in the Phase 2 interviews were asked to complete The Ways of Coping Questionnaire (Revised), an interview schedule previously used with UK parents of a child with Down's syndrome (Knussen *et al.* 1992). Parents are asked to rate how often they use 66 different coping strategies to cope with a problem with their child with disabilities. These 66 questions were reduced into six scales representing different parental coping strategies:

1. Acceptance/positive reappraisal (gaining a positive meaning from having a child with disabilities).

2. Wishful thinking (wishing things were different).

3. Practical coping (trying to directly address the problem).

4. Seeking social support (seeking practical, emotional, information support from others).

5. Cognitive distraction (thinking about something else to take your mind off the problem).

6. Behavioural distraction (doing something else to take your mind off the problem).

Previous research with parents of a child with disabilities (Knussen *et al.* 1992) shows that coping strategies that try to address a problem (practical coping, seeking social support) or find a positive meaning from the problem (acceptance/positive reappraisal) are linked to less parental distress. In contrast, there are a set of coping strategies labelled as emotion-focused (wishful thinking, cognitive distraction, behavioural distraction) which are linked to greater parental distress. This is thought to be because emotion-focused coping strategies are used when a problem is seen as unsolvable; if this is the case, then the only way to manage the stress of the problem is to try and deal with your own emotions about the problem rather than deal with the problem itself.

Parents in the Phase 2 interviews reported using a range of different coping strategies, with no particular coping strategy being used more than others. However, different parents did report very different individual profiles of coping strategies. The only difference between ethnic groups was in practical coping, which Bangladeshi parents reported using most and Indian parents reported using least.

Parents in the Phase 1 interviews also described using a wide range of coping strategies at different stages of the child's life. Some of these, such as acceptance of the child with disabilities, faith, social support from family and friends, and celebration of the child's achievements, were seen as helpful by parents. Others, such as denial of the child's disability, lack of acceptance and support from family and friends, and disappointment in the child's abilities, were seen as unhelpful by parents. For parents in the Phase 1 interviews, different coping strategies were interlinked and had far-reaching effects on parental well-being, the social life of the parent and the child, and the uptake of formal support services.

For example, a lack of parental acceptance of the child's disability could be devastating in its effects on both the child and the family. Wishful thinking could also accompany a lack of acceptance.

> 'What have I done to deserve this?' I told myself. I felt tormented. We were just both [husband and wife] emotional. It was upsetting… We had these feelings inside us all, blocked up inside. Like it went from one stage to another where the child got poorly, needed one operation after another and it was just torment. Nobody being there to support us. The family didn't understand… We [husband and wife] weren't able to talk about it. We just wanted to ignore it so that it never happened… I was too ashamed to talk about it [with anyone] because I never knew anything about disability. We should be, erm, more open with it [the child's disability] to begin with because I regret it. I feel guilty. I had to hide my child and I was ashamed of it. I've got nothing to be ashamed of.
>
> *Firdaus*

> I mean now he's going to be 6 next month, but still. I'm not sure about my husband but it's very hard for me to accept… I won't let that wheelchair come home because in my mind that wheelchair comes home, it's like I'm accepting he's disabled. If he stays in school they use it at school. I mean I know he goes to special school and everything but still in my head I think of it as 'Well, he's only a baby. He's my baby. He's gonna grow out of it'… If he was healthy there would be no problems at all… When I say life would be perfect I mean if he was healthy everything would be OK, but really if I put my mind to it I don't think I could imagine Sayed any different from the way he is.
>
> *Nasreen*

In contrast, many Phase 1 parents reported how their faith had helped them accept their child.

> Yes I do [have concerns for the future], but I also think and satisfy myself that what time has passed for me up till now and God has made it pass by so easily. Then maybe when that time comes, I am worrying at this time, but maybe at that time I won't be as worried. How do I know I may also manage that time so easily, that it would not even affect me. That I'll say

'Oh, I was stupid that I used to think about it for so long that this may happen or that may happen'. I remain dependent on God a lot [laughs].

Zareena

We have to accept the burden and Allah helps you to cope.

Ayesha

I wanted to go there [Pakistan] you know. And go to the worship places there and pray there in my own way to God... And I went everywhere with him... I was thinking in my mind that if I do a lot for him at least I know that I've done something. It helped me a lot.

Amani

Social support from extended family members was also sought by parents when the child with disabilities was accepted by the wider family.

The family members showed him [child with disabilities] a lot of love. They would not let him feel that he was disabled. They would not outcast him because of his disability as happens in a lot of families. He used to stay over at my sister's a lot since the age of 6 months or 1 year. Everyone there gave him a lot of love and attention. He was allowed to do anything as long as it was not wrong, then he would be told not to. He was taught to do everything correctly.

Duaa

[When the parents found out about the child's disability] my parents, they both came down and I just broke down in front of them and they said 'You know, you should get yourself together. He is your child at the end of the day and if he's got a disability you know we love him in every way, but we have to accept him and life goes on. The way you're crying you shouldn't do that because it's gonna be hard for you to help your child. We're gonna help in every way'. They've been very good with him, my sisters, my mum.

Amani

Parental physical health

Systematic research evidence concerning the physical health of UK South Asian parents of a child with severe learning disabilities is lacking, although Hatton *et al.* (1998) reported very high usage of health services among UK South Asian parents of a person with learning disabilities. In the Phase 2

Table 8.1 Physical health problems and use of health services for own health needs: Phase 2 interview parents versus 4th National Survey, by ethnic group

	Our study				4th National Survey (women only)			
	Indian (%)	Pakistani (%)	Bangladeshi (%)	All parents (%)	Indian (%)	Pakistani (%)	Bangladeshi (%)	White (%)
Physical Health Problem								
Self-assessed general health fair/poor/very poor	72	77	43	73	32	38	41	32
Long-standing illness	35	53	50	50	18	20	15	34
Long-standing disability	70	83	60	79	32	39	42	36
Any moderate activities limited by health problems	22	60	67	54	15	24	21	22
Angina or heart attack	0	6.3	13.3	6.6	2.7	3.8	3.7	6.2
Hypertension	10	24	29	22	6	12	11	17
Perceive as too heavy for height	57	40	7	39	23	33	14	47
Diabetes	19	11	14.3	14.7	5.5*	7.6*	7.4*	2.2*
Wheeze or cough up phlegm	22	34	13	29	15	15	12	29
Number of visits to GP in past month								
None	43	31	69	37	59*	51*	55*	66*
1–2	57	44	23	43	33*	38*	36*	30*
3–5	0	21	0	15	7*	10*	7*	4*
>5	0	5	8	5	1*	2*	2*	1*
In-patient hospital stay in past year	19	20	7	19	10*	11*	10*	11*

* 4th National Survey comparison figures for men and women combined

interviews, we asked parents standard questions about physical health taken from the 4th National Survey (Nazroo 1997). This means that physical health problems among parents in our study could be directly compared to larger UK populations taken from the 4th National Survey.

Table 8.1 presents the percentage of physical health problems reported by parents across ethnic groups in the Phase 2 interviews, together with comparative information from the 4th National Survey. To gain the closest possible comparison, information from the 4th National Survey concerning women are presented, as the vast majority of parents in our study were women. There were also no obvious differences in the ages of the parents in our study and participants in the 4th National Survey, so any differences are unlikely to be due to age differences.

As the number of people in our study are relatively small and we are relying on self-report of physical health problems, some caution must be used when looking at Table 8.1. Nevertheless, parents in our study were clearly much more likely to report poor physical health than people in the 4th National Survey across a whole range of physical health problems: self-assessed physical health, long-standing illness and disability, diabetes, respiratory problems, hypertension, angina and heart disease, being overweight, and having moderate activities limited by health problems. Most of these physical health problems were at least twice as common among the parents in the Phase 2 interviews compared to adults from the same ethnic group and White adults in the 4th National Survey.

There were also some differences between ethnic groups in our study, with Bangladeshi parents less likely to assess their health as less than good and less likely to report themselves as overweight. Indian parents were less likely to report that any moderate activities were limited by health problems.

Many parents in the Phase 1 interviews made an explicit link between caring for their child with disabilities and their current physical health problems.

> My own lifestyle has changed a lot because I need help at night...and I feel I would have been better in myself if I hadn't stayed up all night. However, staying awake all night for the sake of the children, for their sickness etc. and having to change their nappies... Because of this I'm ill myself. I have severe arthritis now. Secondly my eyes, my head always aches.
>
> *Zareena*

I have diabetes and a heart condition. I think I'm also ill because of him [child with disabilities]. I can't leave him with anyone, not even for a minute.

Zakiya

I am mostly anxious about the problem of bathing Layla, as I have to take her upstairs by myself and I don't have the facilities that I need... I suffer from backache from picking her up. I fell last year and broke my backbone. I just about manage to take her upstairs now and my daughter-in-law brings her back down.

Huda

In terms of health-related behaviours, parents in the Phase 2 interviews did not report using alcohol (0% of all parents) and were unlikely to be currently smoking (6% of all parents), although use of paan was common among Indian (48%) and Bangladeshi (60%) parents. These figures are broadly comparable to South Asian adults in the 4th National Survey (Nazroo 1997), although the profile of alcohol use (46% in the past week), current smoking (46%) and use of paan (0%) was very different among White adults in the 4th National Survey.

The health needs reported by parents in our study are clearly extensive, and much higher than comparative health needs reported by adults in the 4th National Survey (Nazroo 1997). Unsurprisingly, use of health services for parents' own physical health needs was also greater (see Table 8.1). Overall, 63 per cent of parents had visited their GP in the past month about their own health needs rather than those of their child with disabilities or other family members, a considerably higher number than similar adults in the 4th National Survey. Bangladeshi parents were less likely to have visited their GP than Indian and Pakistani parents. Almost a fifth of parents in the Phase 2 interviews (19%) also reported an in-patient hospital stay for themselves in the past year, again a much higher number than comparative groups. A quarter of these in-patient stays were for childbirth, with in-patient stays ranging from 1 to 15 days. Considering the practical difficulties reported by parents in attending hospital appointments, this extensive use of health services is likely to impose a considerable strain on the management of the family during GP appointments and particularly in-patient hospital stays.

Parental mental health

As mentioned earlier, sparse UK research (Hatton *et al.* 1998) has reported extremely high rates of distress indicative of a mental health problem among South Asian parents of a person with learning disabilities, much higher than comparative UK research using the same interview schedule with mainly White families (Kiernan and Alborz 1994; Sloper *et al.* 1988; Sloper and Turner 1991, 1994). Parents in Phase 2 of our study completed the same interview schedule about parental distress, the Malaise Inventory (Rutter, Tizard and Whitmore 1970) as well as standardised interviews about depression and anxiety used in the 4th National Survey (Nazroo 1998).

Regarding parental distress, overall 74 per cent of Phase 2 parents scored above a threshold on the Malaise Inventory (Rutter *et al.* 1970) which indicates a potential mental health problem. This figure is similar to the 78 per cent of UK South Asian parents of a person with learning disabilities found previously (Hatton *et al.* 1998). It is, however, much higher than the 17 per cent to 67 per cent found in previous UK research with parents of mainly White children with learning disabilities or physical disabilities, including parents of young adults with severely challenging behaviour (Kiernan and Alborz 1994; Sloper *et al.* 1988; Sloper and Turner 1991, 1994). There were no differences between ethnic groups in parental distress.

Figure 8.1 shows that depression (40.4%) and anxiety (26.5%) were much higher among parents in our study compared to adults in the 4th National Survey. Depression among parents was at least ten times more common than among women in the 4th National Survey from the same ethnic group. Indian parents were less likely to be depressed and Pakistani parents most likely to be depressed. Anxiety was at least twice as common for parents in our study compared to women in the 4th National Survey from the same ethnic group. Pakistani parents were most likely to report anxiety and Bangladeshi parents least likely to report anxiety. Although a large proportion of parents in the Phase 2 interviews (42.3%) had spoken to their GP about stress, anxiety or depression in the past month, no parents reported using any kind of mental health service in the past year.

Parents in the Phase 1 interviews described how caring for their child with disabilities without support resulted in emotional distress and more serious mental health problems, such as obsessive-compulsive disorder and attempted suicide.

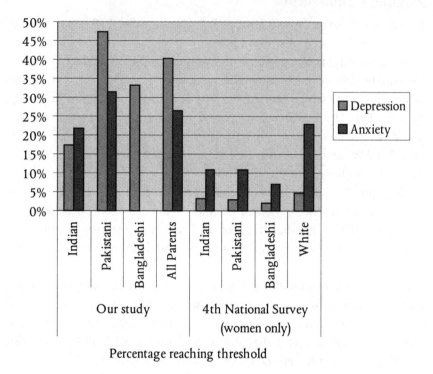

Figure 8.1 Parental depression and anxiety: our study versus 4th National Survey

I am just upset that he [child with disabilities] is ill. I remain upset for him. Only a mother knows how a child is. That is what I am concerned about. Sometimes I will cry and ring my daughter who lives nearby and she talks to me, keeps me happy. My brothers and sisters are in Pakistan. I also pray, but most of the time I cry all the time.

Faiza

Today Iman is feeling well and whatever you give her to eat she will take it and she's happy, but when she's not well then I feel sad because she can't speak. She cannot tell me and she doesn't eat. It's very upsetting.

Azra

All night I have been awake. I have been pacing up and down the stairs. She has a noisy chest. It was because she was in agony, but my mind was going crazy whilst watching and listening to her.

Farida

I worry, have headaches. I take Cocodomal every four hours. Tablets for my heart. I have diabetes. My legs go numb and I have no strength. Believe it or not I was on the settee all day yesterday. He does not sleep. We have to give him medicine in orange juice forcefully. It is very difficult with him to get him to sleep.

Zakiya

I do such things. I've got an obsession, I clean out the kids' bedrooms and they're not allowed to go in the bedrooms until it's bedtime, and wash the carpets. And I'm forever washing the curtains and bedding. And I also take the covers off the sofa and wash them. I don't know I have this cleaning obsession. I'd say it started round about after I had Sayed. It's one thing that I'm in control of.

Nasreen

Even my social workers didn't know what facilities were available for people with learning disabilities. There was nothing on hand at the hospital or the social workers hadn't got time. There was nothing that said that there was any respite care available or anything at all... And it wasn't until I was sat talking to my health visitor... I said 'I'm washing my hands after everything I touch and I'm tidying and I've got to the extent where I'm obsessed now'...and then it came to it that I nearly committed suicide... When I was ready to be discharged the people in the hospital where I had the nervous breakdown they got in contact with the respite care and services for me [upset]. Why couldn't that have been done before?

Firdaus

Summary

Compared to the 4th National Survey (Nazroo 1997, 1998), parents in our study were much more likely to report poor physical health across a whole range of physical health problems: self-assessed physical health, long-standing illness and disability, diabetes, respiratory problems, hypertension, angina and heart disease, being overweight, and having moderate activities limited by health problems. This poor health was reflected by increased use of GP and hospital services. Consumption of alcohol and cigarettes was extremely low among parents, although use of paan was common among Indian and Bangladeshi parents. There were few differences between ethnic groups in self-reported physical health problems.

Rates of distress (74% of parents in the Phase 2 interviews), depression (40.4%) and anxiety (26.5%) were extremely high among parents in our study, with rates of mental health problems up to ten times higher than comparative UK populations (Nazroo 1998) and only matched by a previous UK study of South Asian parents of an adolescent or adult with learning disabilities (Hatton *et al.* 1998). Pakistani parents were more likely to report both anxiety and depression. Despite these high rates of mental health problems, no parents reported using any kind of mental health service in the past year.

Parents in the Phase 1 interviews made explicit links between caring for their child with disabilities, particularly without support, and both physical and mental health problems.

Chapter Nine

Making Connections

The previous chapters have focused in detail on important aspects of the circumstances and experiences of UK South Asian families with a child with severe disabilities: the characteristics of the child, the resources of the family, the disclosure process and information, informal, semi-formal and formal support, the social life of the family, the physical and mental health of parents, and their plans for the future. However, as the quotes from parents in the Phase 1 interviews throughout the book make clear, this division into chapters is in some respects arbitrary, as parents routinely made connections between all these aspects of their circumstances and experiences.

This chapter tries to draw the results of our study together, by examining some of the more important connections between family circumstances and experiences. This is mainly done using multivariate statistics (multiple regression and logistic regression) conducted on information from the Phase 2 interviews. Full details of the statistical methods are available in Hatton *et al.* (2002); the purpose of the statistics was to find which factors were most closely linked to important family outcomes such as parental health, family social life, and support from family, friends and services.

Because we only have information from parents at one point in time, we have to be careful when talking about certain factors predicting or causing important outcomes for families. However, parents in the Phase 1 and Phase 3 interviews had strong ideas about which factors caused important family outcomes. In fact, there was high agreement between the statistical analyses and the views of parents expressed in Phases 1 and 3; this increases our confidence that our findings are accurate.

Factors linked to parental health

Figure 9.1 presents a summary in diagram form of the statistical analyses, showing the most important factors linked to parental physical and mental health. This diagram raises several important issues, also mentioned by parents in the Phase 1 and Phase 3 interviews.

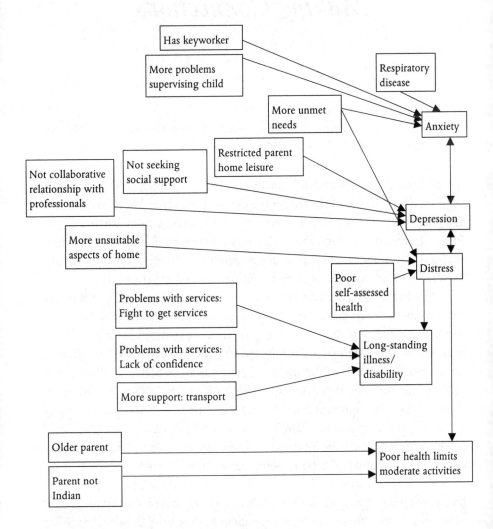

Figure 9.1 Factors linked to parental health

First, it is clear that parental physical and mental health problems, at least as reported by parents, are linked to each other. In particular, anxiety and distress were linked to respiratory health problems, poor self-assessed health, long-standing illness or disability, and health limitations on moderate activities. Depression, although linked to anxiety and distress, was not linked to physical health problems. In the Phase 1 interviews (see Chapter 8), several parents reported that their physical health problems made them more anxious about the care of their child. In a vicious circle, these parents also reported that their anxiety and distress made them physically ill. Although parents reported increased use of general health services, particularly GP services, this did not result in parents receiving help for mental health problems. These results suggest that attempts to relieve parents' physical health problems in isolation are unlikely to be effective without also paying attention to the mental health needs of parents. Of course, support in relieving parental mental health problems requires easily accessible and non-stigmatising support services.

Second, parental physical health problems were linked to struggles with services for their child with disabilities. Parents with long-standing illness or disability, although receiving more help with transport from family or friends, also reported a lack of confidence in service professionals and a constant fight to get services. As reported above, many parents find access to services arduous, and often the product of long struggles with services. It is likely that parental illness or disability makes these struggles for services worse, resulting in a lack of confidence in professionals. More health limitations on moderate activities by parents were linked to greater parental age, confirming the experiences of older parents in the Phase 1 interviews that they require more practical support as their child gets older. In addition, Indian parents were less likely to report limitations on moderate activities, reflecting statistics from the 4th National Survey (see Nazroo 1997 and Table 8.1).

Third, parental depression was linked to similar factors to those found in previous studies concerning parents of children with disabilities across ethnic groups (see Hatton 2002 for a summary). In our study, restricted home leisure for parents, parents not seeking social support as a coping strategy, and parents not having a collaborative relationship with professionals are linked to parental depression. These factors suggest something of a vicious circle for depressed parents, as suggested by some parents in the Phase 1 interviews. A lack of a collaborative relationship with professionals is linked to parental depression, which in turn is linked to restrictions in parental activities and parents not seeking social support to relieve their depression. Depressed parents may therefore become isolated from informal and formal sources of support, unless service professionals across a range of agencies are alert to potential depression in parents and proactive in helping parents to gain support.

Fourth, anxiety and distress were linked to similar factors, mainly a greater number of unmet family needs but also more unsuitable housing and more problems with supervising their child with disabilities. Unsurprisingly, parents were anxious when the basic needs of their child were not met and the home was seen as unsuitable, with obvious implications for service supports. Parents were also anxious if they found supervising their child more of a problem; again, service support both within the home and with leisure activities of the child outside the home could be useful in relieving parental anxiety. In addition, anxious parents were more likely to report having a keyworker, possibly because, as some of the Phase 1 and Phase 3 parents identified, keyworkers were sometimes assigned to parents only when the parent had reached some kind of crisis point. Given the general supportiveness of keyworkers reported by parents in all the interview phases, the routine assignment of keyworkers to families would appear to be preferable to crisis-driven assignment.

Finally, with the exception of limitations on moderate activities, it is worth noting, along with Nazroo (1997, 1998), that there were very few ethnic differences in parental health once other factors had been taken into account. This suggests that the factors that cause poor physical and mental health are similar across ethnic groups, although different ethnic groups experience different levels of risk, resulting in different profiles of physical and mental health problems across ethnic groups.

Factors linked to family social life, unmet family needs and satisfaction with services

Figure 9.2 presents a summary in diagram form of the statistical analyses, showing all the factors most closely linked to parent and child social life, unmet needs, and parental satisfaction with service supports generally.

Parents reported more restrictions on their own social lives if they had more unmet needs and if they reported more problems with supervising their child with disabilities. Both these factors were also associated with parental anxiety, highlighting the wide-ranging influence of child and family needs on outcomes for parents.

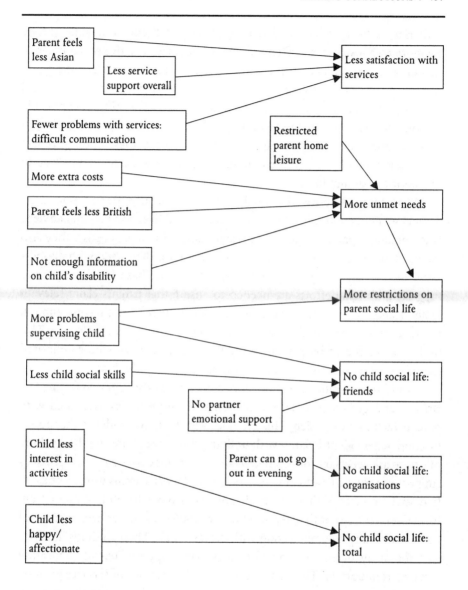

Figure 9.2 Factors linked to social life, unmet needs, service satisfaction

The social life of the child was mainly associated with child characteristics, with a more active social life associated with greater child social skills, the child being more interested in activities, the child being more happy/affectionate, and parents reporting fewer problems with supervising their child. As parents in the Phase 1 interviews reported, this link may work both ways; the child is more likely to have an active social life with friends and family if they are more responsive to social environments, but also an active social life may encourage improvements in the child's social skills. It is worth noting that child involvement in organisations was not linked to child characteristics, and was only linked to parents being able to go out in the evening. It is possible that organisations are equally accepting of the child no matter what their level of social responsiveness, although it is more likely that these findings reflect the very low number of children in our study who were actually involved in organisations of any kind.

As mentioned above, the number of unmet family needs reported by parents was linked to restrictions in parents' social lives and parental anxiety. Unsurprisingly, parents reported a greater number of unmet needs if they also reported more extra costs associated with caring for their child with disabilities. This message was reinforced by parents in the Phase 1 interviews, and suggests additional efforts are needed to ensure that parents claim relevant benefits and have access to specialist equipment. Parents not having enough information on the child's disability also reported more unmet needs. This finding is reinforced by parents in the Phase 1 interviews, who emphasised the importance of accurate information on the child's disability.

In addition, parents reporting more unmet needs also reported feeling less British, and greater parental satisfaction with services was associated with parents feeling more Asian. This provides very tentative evidence that acculturation, where identification with both the majority culture and their culture of origin are necessary for positive acculturation, may have a role in accessing supportive services (Hatton in press; Newland 1999). Parents were more satisfied with services if they received more (and more helpful) support from formal services, and if they reported fewer problems with services in terms of having difficulty communicating with professionals. These findings illustrate that for many parents the quantity of service supports, outside education services, is important. They also illustrate the importance of services possessing the linguistic competence to communicate effectively with South Asian parents.

Factors linked to support

Figure 9.3 presents a summary in diagram form of the statistical analyses, showing the most important factors linked to support from formal (services), semi-formal (parent groups, etc.) and informal (family, friends, etc.) sources.

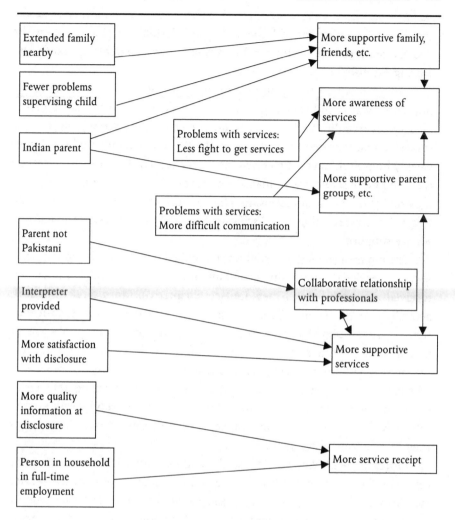

Figure 9.3 Factors linked to support

As parents in the Phase 1 interviews noted, there were important links between informal, semi-formal and formal supports. Parents were aware of a wider range of services if they received more informal and semi-formal support, suggesting that information on available services was coming largely from these sources rather than professionals. Where parents were aware of more services they reported fewer problems in having to fight to get services, although they reported more problems in terms of difficulties in communicating with professionals. As suggested earlier, increased parental awareness of services does not necessarily translate into increased service support, with communication barriers perhaps one reason for this. These findings correspond to a certain extent with the findings of Hatton *et al.* (1998), where the two factors associated with service awareness were parents speaking and writing English.

Parents reported receiving a wider range of services if someone in the household was in full-time employment. This evidence for inverse targeting by services (families with more resources receive more service supports) is similar to that reported by Hatton *et al.* (1998), where families with a higher weekly household income received more services. Furthermore, in our study receiving more services was linked to better quality information having been provided at the point of disclosure. This supports the views of parents in the Phase 1 interviews that the disclosure process has a long-term impact on service supports.

The range of services received was not linked to the Family Support Scale index of service support, which combines information on which services are received and how helpful they are (see Chapter 6). More service support, according to the Family Support Scale, was linked to more semi-formal support, suggesting that these sources of support (particularly in terms of parent support groups) may mutually reinforce each other. However, there was no link with informal support; informal supports generally do not seem to help parents in accessing service supports, and service supports do not seem to be targeted at parents without informal supports. Clearly, service supports are relatively insensitive to the circumstances of families in terms of the supports they receive from other sources.

Other factors linked to the quantity and helpfulness of service supports reinforce the importance of disclosure and communication. Greater service support was linked to greater parent satisfaction with the disclosure process, again emphasising the long-term impact of disclosure. More service support was also linked to having access to an interpreter, again emphasising the importance of good communication in accessing service supports and ensuring that they are useful to parents. Finally, families receiving greater service support also reported having a collaborative relationship with professionals. This collaborative relationship with professionals, linked to low parental depression, was itself linked to greater formal service support and the parent not being Pakistani. This suggests that Pakistani families may be less likely to be accessing formal service supports due to poor relationships with professionals.

The quantity and helpfulness of semi-formal support (parent groups, etc.) was only linked to the quantity and helpfulness of service supports and parents being Indian. Indian parents were more likely to access semi-formal supports, possibly helping to raise awareness and access to service supports.

Indian parents were also more likely to receive more (and more helpful) informal support from family and friends. As with living circumstances in the UK generally (Modood *et al.* 1997), Indian families appear to be more successful in accessing informal and semi-formal supports than Pakistani and Bangladeshi families, although this does not translate into greater access to service supports. Unsurprisingly, parents were more likely to receive informal support if they had extended family living nearby, confirming the views of parents in the Phase 1 interviews. Parents were also more likely to receive informal support if they had fewer problems supervising their child. Parents in the Phase 1 interviews suggested that this link may work both ways, with more informal support helping them to manage the supervision of their child, but also extended families and friends being more likely to help if the child was more able, socially responsive and showed fewer problem behaviours. From these results, it appears that, irrespective of the level of informal support, sustained formal support from services is needed for families.

Making connections

To help interpret the wealth of findings arising from our study, Figure 9.4 presents a map of the most important linkages we found in the study, drawing on the reports of parents across all phases of the project. This map can be briefly summarised as follows.

First, the disclosure process, itself influenced by the time of diagnosis and parental concerns about the child, is crucial for parents. A well-conducted disclosure process (giving clear information in the appropriate language to both parents in an emotionally supportive way) helps parents to accept their child's disability and mobilise formal support services. Parental acceptance helps extended family and friends to accept the child. This, if extended families also live nearby and are able to help, is likely to lead to informal support for parents. More able and socially responsive children with disabilities, with fewer problem behaviours, are also likely to attract more informal support.

This informal support, together with information from parent support groups and greater parental acceptance and understanding of the child's disability, helps parents to become aware of and mobilise formal service supports. The cultural identity of parents may also play a role in the mobilisation of formal service supports. This mobilisation also requires appropriate language support, a trusted professional in a keyworker role and a collaborative relationship between parents and professionals in order to translate parental

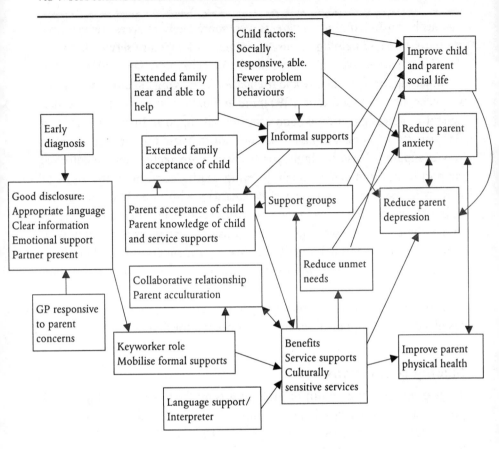

Figure 9.4 Map of the main findings of the study

awareness of services into the uptake of benefits and a greater range and quantity of helpful services.

Service supports, particularly when culturally sensitive, reinforce the collaborative relationship between parents and professionals, put parents in contact with support groups, reduce the unmet needs of families and help to improve the physical health of parents. In contrast, informal supports and parent support groups help to improve the social life of the child and the family, especially when the child is socially responsive and more family needs are being met.

Informal supports, along with formal service supports and an active family social life, also help to reduce parental depression. Parental distress and anxiety are more likely to be relieved if more of the family's needs are being met, the child is less of a problem to supervise, and the parent has fewer physical health problems.

Chapter Ten

Conclusions

Our study has tried to provide a rich picture of the circumstances and experiences of South Asian families with a child with severe disabilities. Extensive survey interviews and repeated in-depth interviews with parents have produced a consistent picture of families often desperately needing support from services but rarely receiving support that is sufficient and helpful to families. This lack of service support can have a serious impact on the whole family, making South Asian families with a child with severe disabilities an urgent priority group for service improvements and policy initiatives. As the findings from our study are complex, this final chapter will begin by summarising the major findings of our study. The chapter will then discuss some of the major issues arising from conducting research with the families in our study, and the implications of our study for policy and practice.

The findings

Financial resources

As with previous research, parents in our study reported a pattern of pervasive material disadvantage. Household income was low (median £100 to £199 weekly), unemployment was high (54.5% of households had no one in full-time employment), and the patchy uptake of benefits was insufficient to meet the extra costs of caring for the child with disabilities.

Housing

Housing was generally rated as unsuitable for the needs of the child, particularly in terms of lack of space and safety issues. Adaptations to housing were rare, often delayed, and sometimes insensitive to the cultural needs of the family.

Main carer

Most main carers were mothers born outside the UK, but who had spent many years in the UK and cared for the family full time. Substantial numbers of families had a lone parent (12%) or were caring for more than one person with disabilities (21%), more than UK families in previous research. Only a minority of main carers could speak, read or write English, with parents reporting a wide variety of spoken and written languages. Almost all main carers were Muslim (93.4%).

The child with disabilities

Children in our study covered a wide age range, with a slight majority of boys. Most parents described their child as having unspecified learning disabilities, with rare reporting of specific conditions. Most children needed substantial support across a range of self-care skills, household tasks and spoken communication skills. Most parents described their children as fairly happy, sociable and affectionate, but over 80 per cent of parents also reported problems associated with eating, toileting and bedtime routines, and their child throwing things, yelling, screaming and throwing tantrums. Around half of parents felt their child had made progress in the past six months, with most parents appearing to adjust their expectations to the skills and progress for the child, enabling the family to recognise and celebrate the child's achievements.

Disclosure

Most children were diagnosed as having a disability by 4 years of age. Disclosure was mostly conducted by a medical professional in English. Around half of parents reported understanding what was told to them at disclosure, with most receiving good support from partners and the disclosing professional. Post-disclosure support was, however, lacking. Parents reported the following factors as essential for parental satisfaction with disclosure: prompt disclosure in the appropriate language with the partner present; emotional support; and clear and practical information linked to action to gain service supports. For parents, a well-conducted disclosure process could have long-term positive consequences, such as increased parental understanding and acceptance of the child, and the mobilising of informal and formal supports.

Information

Many parents reported having enough information about the child's disability, although fewer parents had enough information about services for the child or for themselves as parents. Parents using the English language were more likely to report having enough information. Parents also reported preferring to receive information in the appropriate language from a professional face-to-face.

Informal support

The most common source of informal support for parents was within the household. Partners usually provided both practical and emotional support, and absent or unsupportive partners could result in practical difficulties and emotional distress. Practical support from other children in the household was also seen as helpful by most parents, although parents reported concerns about the impact of caring responsibilities on these children. Few parents reported receiving support from extended families or religious organisations. This was partly due to extended family members living too far away or being unable to provide support, although even when received this support was often rated as unhelpful.

Formal support: awareness and uptake

As with previous research, parents generally reported high awareness of generic health and welfare services and special education services, but low awareness of other specialist disability services. Uptake of specialist services, with the exception of GP and school services, was generally low. Indian parents and parents who used English reported greater awareness and uptake of services. Although many parents reported racism and discrimination within services, this was not always from White professionals. Parents also strongly preferred integrated services that routinely met their child's language, cultural and religious needs rather than ethnically separate services.

Formal support: relationships with professionals

Less than half of parents reported collaborative relationships with professionals. Problems with services experienced by most parents included communication barriers and constant fighting to gain service support, resulting in parental frustration and lack of confidence in services. Bangladeshi parents reported fewer problems with services, possibly due to lower expectations of services, and Indian parents reported more problems with services. English language use was associated with less fighting to get services.

Formal support: schools

Almost all children were in special schools, which were generally very highly rated by parents. Parents reported that special schools were good for the child, gave parents a break, were responsive to their concerns, and were often the only reliable point of contact with services to gain information and support. However, very few schools were reported to provide for the language, cultural or religious needs of the children, and parents were also concerned about the availability and quality of speech therapy and physiotherapy. A small number of parents reported dissatisfaction with special schools in terms of poor standards of care and lack of parental choice.

Formal support: respite services

Few parents reported awareness and uptake of respite care services for their child. Almost all respite care received was in respite units managed by social services. These services were generally highly valued and responsive to the child's cultural needs, but insufficient for parental needs.

Formal support: interpreters

Although most parents reported needing an interpreter, less than half had been provided with one. Where used, interpreters were highly valued, with parents particularly appreciating being able to say what they wanted confidentially without having to rely on family or friends for interpretation. Parents who had not used an interpreter reported most commonly relying on their partner or another child in the family for help with interpreting.

Formal support: family support groups

Few parents reported being aware of or participating in family support groups. Parents valued the information function of these groups and the chance to meet other parents to gain emotional support. However, the helpfulness of these groups to parents was limited, possibly because attendance did not result in increased service support.

Formal support: keyworker

A minority of parents (28%) reported having a keyworker, with social workers and health visitors often taking on a keyworker role. Where provided, keyworkers were almost always viewed as invaluable, in terms of raising parental awareness of benefits and services, organising integrated packages of care, and providing ongoing emotional support.

Formal support: unmet needs

The range of unmet needs reported by parents was extremely high, substantially higher than those reported in comparable UK research. Bangladeshi parents reported lower unmet needs in a range of areas, and Pakistani parents reported greater unmet needs in emergency health and child care.

The relationship between formal and informal support

For most parents formal support services were needed to compensate for a lack of informal supports. Few parents reported complementary or collaborative relationships between informal and formal supports, with some parents reporting no emotional support from any source.

Future plans for the child

Few parents had considered or discussed future plans for the child. Parents with a child about to leave school reported considerable uncertainty and confusion about the post-education service supports available. Parents who had been in contact with adult services reported concerns about the cultural and religious appropriateness of the services offered. Parents of older girls were particularly concerned about same-sex personal care for their child.

Social life of parents

Parents reported wide-ranging restrictions on their social and leisure activities, including nights out and weekends away, restrictions reported by a greater number of Pakistani families. These restrictions were exacerbated if the child required constant supervision and if the family was headed by a single parent. Reliable informal and formal supports outside school hours helped parents to have an active social life.

Social life of the child

The social life of the child with disabilities was similarly restricted, with the vast majority of children having no social involvement with friends or organised activities. Most parents were unhappy with their child's social life, which was particularly restricted if the extended family and the general public held negative attitudes towards the child.

Parental health

Compared to national surveys, parents in our study were much more likely to report poor physical health across a whole range of physical health problems. This poor health was reflected by increased use of GP and hospital services. Rates of distress (74% of Phase 2 parents), depression (40.4%) and anxiety (26.5%) were extremely high among the parents in our study, up to ten times higher than comparative UK populations. Pakistani parents were more likely to report both anxiety and depression. Despite these high rates of mental health problems, no parents reported using any kind of mental health service for themselves in the past year. Parents made explicit links between caring for their child with disabilities, particularly without support, and physical and mental health problems.

Factors associated with positive family outcomes

Several factors emerged as central in promoting positive outcomes for families.

First, the disclosure process, itself influenced by the time of diagnosis and parental concerns about the child, was crucial for parents. A well-conducted disclosure process helped parents to accept the child's disability, access formal support services and take up benefits. Parental acceptance also helped acceptance by extended family and friends which, if extended families were able to help, was likely to lead to informal support for parents. More able and socially responsive children with disabilities, with fewer problem behaviours, were also likely to receive more informal support.

Second, informal support, together with information from parent support groups and greater parental acceptance and understanding of the child's disability, helped parents to become aware of and access formal service supports. The cultural identity of parents may also have played a role in actively seeking formal service supports. This active uptake of services also required language support (for example interpreters), a trusted keyworker and a collaborative relationship between parents and professionals to translate parental awareness of services into the uptake of benefits and services.

Third, culturally sensitive services reinforced collaborative relationships between parents and professionals, put parents in contact with support groups, reduced the unmet needs of families and helped to improve the physical health of parents. Informal supports and parent support groups helped to improve the social life of the child and the family, especially when the child was socially responsive and more family needs were being met.

Finally, informal supports, along with formal service supports and an active family social life, also helped to reduce parental depression. Parental distress and anxiety were more likely to be relieved if the family's needs were being met, the child was less of a problem to supervise, and the parent had fewer physical health problems.

Researching with families

Before discussing the implications of our study for policy-makers, we want to highlight some broader issues raised by our study, particularly the value of research studies like this one and general issues involved in conducting cross-cultural research, including the implications of these issues for services.

Participants versus participatory research

Our study has tried to build a rich picture of the lives of South Asian families with a child with severe disabilities. The methods we used were designed to involve parents in the research process and to give parents some influence over how we carried out the study. For example, the interview schedules used in the Phase 2 interviews were partly chosen depending on what parents in the open-ended Phase 1 interviews told us was important. Particular Phase 2 interview schedules were also checked out with parents in later Phase 1 interviews. In the Phase 3 interviews we checked out with parents our interpretations of the findings from the Phase 1 and Phase 2 interviews. We hope that this book reflects the experiences of parents, and that the voices of the parents come through as a central aspect of our study.

However, we do recognise that the involvement of parents in the research process was limited and falls far short of recommendations made for participatory research (Ramcharan, Grant and Flynn in press). Participatory research is a way of doing research that includes people on the receiving end of the study as joint researchers. Ideally, this involves people in deciding what the research should be about, how the research is done, how the research is analysed, what it means, and how the findings of the study should be shared. Our study falls even further short of the recommendations of emancipatory research (Ramcharan *et al.* in press), where people normally on the receiving end of research also control the research funding and who does the research.

Given the often desperate circumstances of families in our study, it is not clear that families would have used the project's funding for research at all, and would have preferred the funding to go to direct service support (see the final quote at the end of this chapter). This understandable scepticism about the value of research is borne out by the fact that the failure of services to meet the needs of people with learning disabilities from South Asian communities has been highlighted repeatedly for over a decade (Baxter *et al.* 1990), with little evidence that services have radically improved over time. This strongly suggests a role for future action-oriented research, where families are in control of action research budgets that implement service changes and evaluate their effectiveness.

Cross-cultural research

Our study has used cross-cultural research methods to explore similarities and differences between South Asian families across ethnic communities (Indian, Pakistani and Bangladeshi). Cross-cultural methods have also been used to compare families in this study to other people in previous work, particularly families with a child with severe disabilities, across a wide range of ethnic groups (Beresford 1995; Chamba *et al.* 1999). The methods we have used assume that it is possible to compare the experiences of cultural groups, using a common set of interviews expressing the same ideas (for example, parental depression and distress). However, within the social sciences generally, there are very different views on whether cross-cultural research should be done at all. Social science theorists (see Berry *et al.* 2002) have identified three major stances on cross-cultural research.

The first major stance has been labelled absolutism (Berry *et al.* 2002). This stance assumes that people are fundamentally the same across all cultures. Culture is assumed to play little or no role in how people think, feel or behave. According to this stance, once an idea (and a way of assessing it) has been developed for one culture, it is in principle easy to export to all other cultures, once technical issues such as translatability have been sorted out. By default, almost all research with people with learning disabilities has taken this abso-lutist stance (Hatton in press), by conducting research almost exclusively with White communities and assuming that the findings apply across the board. As our study and many others have shown, services also generally take this stance, by assuming that services designed for White English speakers are equally accessible to everyone. The parents in our study have clearly shown that an absolutist stance does not work for them, in that culture is an important influence on their experiences and services designed for White English speakers clearly are neither accessible nor useful.

In direct contrast to this is a second stance described as relativist (Berry *et al.* 2002). This stance assumes that all human experiences are determined by culture. This means that the world views of each culture are unique, and cannot be understood by reference to the world views of any other culture. Taking this stance, all research should be about building up a rich picture of each culture individually in order to understand that culture 'on its own terms'. There is therefore no point in trying to compare cultures, as there is no common frame of reference with which to do this. The findings of our study do not support this view. For example, parents in our study made many references to similarities between their experiences and those of parents from other ethnic groups. In addition, most of the factors associated with positive outcomes for families in our study (see Chapter 9) are similar to the factors emerging in previous studies of families with a child with learning disabilities in other cultural groups (Blacher 2001; Hatton 2002). These findings suggest that there are some commonalities in the experiences of families with a child with disabilities across ethnic communities.

Our study lends most support to the third stance mentioned by social scientists which is called universalism (Berry *et al.* 2002). This stance assumes that basic aspects of human experience are universal, but that a person's culture will influence how these basic aspects of human experience are displayed. According to this view, we cannot know in advance what aspects of human experience will turn out to be the same across cultures, and what aspects of human experience will be strongly influenced by culture. Careful cross-cultural research is needed to find answers to these questions. Our study strongly supports the idea that there are basic human experiences and that these experiences will be strongly influenced by culture.

For example, in Chapter 4 parents identified a number of aspects of good practice in disclosure. These are similar to good practice guidelines drawn up for White parents (see Sloper and Turner 1993; Turner and Sloper 1992), except that the issue of language came up as very important in our study. This issue has not arisen in previous research, as parents and professionals have always spoken the same language (English). Around the time of disclosure, it also seems that parents across cultures are trying to meet the same two broad challenges, described in previous work as trying to find meaning in the child's disability and accepting the child, and facing practical challenges in making day-to-day adaptations to the child's disability (Floyd *et al.* 1996). However, the way that parents meet these challenges seems to be strongly influenced by culture, for example in the ways that parents look for a meaning in their child's disability.

Another example concerns short-term care/respite care (see Chapter 6). Here, parents in our study report many similar concerns to those expressed by parents across a range of ethnic groups (Beresford 1995; Chamba *et al.* 1999), and also identify many similar requirements for good practice in respite care. However, parents in our study identified some extra requirements for good practice respite care that may apply across cultures, including the need for respite carers who speak the same language as the parents and the need for same-sex carers for intimate personal care tasks. There may also be cultural influences on how respite care is used, for example in terms of what activities the child will enjoy and in terms of patterns of respite care use.

A universalist service?

The stance of social scientists called universalism discussed in the previous section might also be a useful framework for services. This framework would have several advantages over the way that services currently work.

First, such a framework does not make any assumptions about families. At present, services seem to largely operate a 'colour-blind' approach, where services for White English-speaking families are seen as the default option, and the inadequacy of these services for families from South Asian communities is blamed on these families, who are seen as awkward or wanting something extra. At the opposite extreme, a service might assume that a person's culture is the only relevant factor to take into account when designing a service, possibly leading to specialist services based on ethnic stereotypes and the service ignoring economic disadvantage. A service adopting a universalist framework would not make any assumptions about how culture influences the service needs of individual families.

Second, this framework highlights the importance of racism and discrimination, while recognising that this is a complex issue for many families. In our study many parents identified direct racism and discrimination as reasons for not receiving appropriate services, and most parents identified the cultural inappropriateness of services as reasons for not using them (Chapter 6).

Although some parents felt discriminated against by White professionals, other parents felt discriminated against by some South Asian professionals (Chapter 6), suggesting that racism and discrimination may be complex issues that interact with social class and gender issues for some families.

Third, this framework does not forget the fundamental importance of poor housing, unemployment, low income and poor health, and would work to address these fundamentally economic problems for all families in need.

Finally, services adopting this framework would focus on the needs of individual families as expressed by families themselves. This should lead to all services routinely meeting the language, cultural and religious needs of families within mainstream services, the preference strongly expressed by families in our study. Services would adopt this approach with all families, including White families (who also have ethnicity and culture).

Lessons for policy and practice

As discussed in Chapter 1, three current policy initiatives are particularly relevant to South Asian families with a child with severe disabilities: the National Carers Strategy; the Quality Protects initiative; and Valuing People. These three policy initiatives have consistent aims, including improving services for people with disabilities and their carers from minority ethnic groups. This section will briefly outline the most important lessons from our study for current policy initiatives, by focusing on issues identified as crucial either by our study or by government.

Improving the material circumstances of families

A striking feature of our study is the disadvantage experienced by families in housing, employment and income. Although improving access to benefits would help many South Asian families, many families reported that benefits were not enough to cover the extra costs of caring for a child with severe disabilities, particularly in the context of high unemployment. Charging for services is likely to have a disproportionate impact on uptake among South Asian families. As well as increasing financial support, an additional priority should be the rapid provision of aids and adaptations, from specialist nappies through to wheelchairs and housing adaptations, based on a thorough assessment of family needs, including cultural and religious needs.

Improving information for families

Although current policy initiatives emphasise the importance of information, strategic recommendations such as a charter, NHS Direct helplines or websites are unlikely to be used by South Asian families with a child with severe disabilities. These families reported wanting to receive information face-to-face in their preferred language. A well-conducted disclosure process, co-ordinated with ongoing keyworker support and the encouragement of family support groups, would seem to be necessary for increasing parental acceptance and understanding of their child's condition. This parental acceptance and understanding is itself necessary for the family to access informal and formal supports. For families already in the system, ongoing informational support from a keyworker is a priority.

Assessments of family needs

All the current policy initiatives emphasise the importance of fast, comprehensive and regular assessments of family needs. The parents in our study rarely reported receiving such assessments, resulting in service supports often being absent, patchy, unco-ordinated or unhelpful. For assessments to be helpful to South Asian families, they must be conducted in the preferred language of the parent, be relevant to the parents' circumstances, be quickly followed by concrete action, and be regularly updated. Again, a trusted keyworker would be in a good position to perform assessments. In assessment, it is important to avoid both 'colour-blindness' (assuming that equality means offering the same service to everyone, even if it is inaccessible and inappropriate for some groups) and stereotyping on the basis of parental ethnicity or religion (assuming that all families from the same ethnic group will require exactly the same service without assessing individual needs and preferences). Both of these stances do not involve the assessment of individual family needs and preferences and should be avoided.

Co-ordinated packages of care

Like previous research, our study has demonstrated an often desperate need for service supports among South Asian families with a child with severe disabilities, especially as informal supports are uncommon. However, it is clear from our study that comprehensive and co-ordinated packages of care for South Asian families are extremely rare. Except for special education, family support services are rarely used and are often viewed as so unhelpful that they are discontinued. Again, a keyworker would be invaluable to co-ordinate services. To provide co-ordinated packages of care that genuinely meet the needs of families will require a substantial increase in resources and much greater creativity on the part of service agencies to provide 'person-centred' supports, rather than fitting families into pre-existing service slots that are likely to be particularly unhelpful for South Asian families.

Meeting language, cultural and religious needs

Again in common with previous research, our study has shown that few services meet the language, cultural and religious needs of South Asian families. The recruitment and retention of South Asian staff throughout main-stream services for people with learning disabilities should be a priority, as should the expansion of specialist interpreting services trained to deal with disability issues. Greater priority should be given to meeting the cultural and religious needs of all people with disabilities and their families, including appropriate diet, celebration of religious festivals and same-sex carers for intimate personal care tasks. Finally, it should be noted that parents in our study would prefer ethnically integrated services that routinely meet the cultural and religious needs of the child with disabilities, rather than ethnically separate services.

Choice, control and consultation

The importance of choice, control and consultation is being emphasised in current policy initiatives. However, there was very little evidence of families being consulted about services, or of parents having substantial choice or control over the service supports provided. On a service planning level, mean-ingful consultation would involve encouraging the formation of parent support groups, although services would have to show some quick changes in response to parental suggestions for parents to keep attending. Person-centred planning assessment processes, along with greater flexibility and creativity in service supports, could help families to gain more control over family support services.

Meeting the needs of the child with disabilities

Objectives of current policy initiatives include maximising the achievements of the child through education, encouraging children to be fit and healthy, and ensuring that children lead a normal life. Parents in our study highly valued special education services and mostly felt that their child was making progress, despite substantial support needs and high levels of problem behaviour. As these characteristics of the child influence levels of informal support and parental mental health, more intensive early intervention could have a broader impact upon the family as a whole. The provision of some teaching in the family language of the child, together with more reliable and helpful speech therapy and physiotherapy, were also indicated as priorities by parents. Finally, the extreme social isolation of the children in our study is worth noting as a priority for services.

Meeting the needs of parents

The National Carers Strategy emphasises the importance of ensuring that services enable parents to live a full life, maintain paid employment if desired, maintain their physical and mental health, and integrate into local communities. The parents in our study are clearly a priority group for all these objectives. Parents reported their lives revolving around caring for their child with disabilities, extremely restricted social lives, and extremely poor physical and mental health. Although most main carers in our study did not report a wish to go into paid employment, high rates of household unemployment suggest that this could be a priority for their partners. Clearly, the provision of flexible, reliable, sufficient and culturally appropriate short-term care services is crucial here. Many parents also suggested the idea of drop-in centres where children could be left out of school hours. The provision of reliable schemes during school holidays is also vital for parents, as current support is absent or largely unhelpful. For the parents in our study, improving their physical and mental health was closely tied to improving supports for the whole family. However, despite parents' high use of GP and hospital services, no parents reported receiving help for mental health problems. Given the extremely high rates of distress, anxiety and depression, this issue should be addressed urgently.

Inclusion

Current policy stresses the importance of inclusion philosophies for families with a child with disabilities. Reforming education services is an important part of inclusion ideologies, with services shifting from special schools to children with disabilities being educated in mainstream education services with support. While parents in our study were broadly supportive of integrated services, they were also highly appreciative of special schools. These provided a reliable, high-quality service, and also often served as parents' only point of access to other parents and information about other services. Any moves towards mainstreaming children with severe disabilities need to ensure that educational standards are maintained. Furthermore, effective alternatives in terms of supporting and providing information to parents need to be in place before mainstreaming occurs.

Transition

While transition plans for children with disabilities aged 14 and over are a current policy, no parent in our study reported being aware of a transition plan for their teenager. However, transition plans are urgently required, as parents reported great uncertainty and anxiety about services for their child after education stopped. Greater consistency between child and adult services is also required, as some parents reported that adult services that had been offered to them did not meet the language, cultural or religious needs of their child.

Joined-up thinking

Although in this section we have focused on specific policies, it is important to note that the parents in our study consistently reported that support services should meet the needs of the whole family, with child supports having a positive impact on parents and vice versa. Furthermore, the circumstances of the families in our study have wider implications for broader policy initiatives. For example, these families would appear to be priorities for the Children's National Service Framework, the National Service Framework for Mental Health, and the Children's Fund dedicated to eliminating child poverty. Policy-makers and commissioners need to harness and co-ordinate resources from this array of policy initiatives to meet the needs of families. Such 'joined-up thinking' is necessary if the often desperate circumstances and lives of South Asian families with a child with severe disabilities are to be transformed.

In keeping with the general spirit of our study, we would like the last word to go to a parent. Although to some extent we share her scepticism about the impact of research on policy, we hope that on this occasion we are proved wrong by the actions of government and service agencies.

> I mean I don't know how much money the council or the government has funded into this project…all right yes do your research as well, but it would be nice if they took some of that money and put it into projects that parents were – 'cos it's all about children with learning disabilities… Loads of people have come. Somebody's researching this and somebody's researching that. It would be nice if they actually, instead of using

all this money on just doing research. Like I know maybe at the end of the day it does help, but it would be nice if they got some of it and put it into something that benefited these children.

Nasreen

Appendix 1

Probe Questions
for Phase 1 Interviews

1. Basic information, including parent and child age and gender, ethnicity and religion, number of people in household with and without learning disabilities, preferred spoken and written language(s).

2. Any questions for the interviewer about the research project or the interview?

3. Would you like to tell me about your child?

4. Why do you think your child is at [name of education service]?

5. When did you first notice that something was different about your child?

6. How did you understand this difference? *(Probe for labels/understanding of disability issues)*

7. When did you find out about the disability? Who told you?

8. How did you feel about the way that you were told?

9. How did your family and friends react? What kind of things did you tell yourselves?

10. Could anything have been done to make the telling easier?

11. Who helped you at this time? In what ways?

12. Were you satisfied with this help?

13. Is there any other help that you would have liked to have had?

14. In what way would things be different for you if your child was not in [name of education service]? *(Probe for differences if child did not have a learning disability)*

15. *(If more than one child with learning disabilities)* How has the experience with [name of child with learning disabilities] been different from [name of other children with learning disabilities]?

16. How does the child fit into the family? *(Probe for influence on family life)*

17. How does the rest of the family react to your child? *(Probe on spouse, sibling reactions)*

18. Could you describe a typical good day? *(Probe for weekday and weekend)*

19. Could you describe a typical bad day? *(Probe for weekday and weekend)*

20. Could you tell me about your social life and interests? *(Probe for family social life and interests).*

21. What activities do you enjoy doing with your child? *(Additional probe question:* What do you do when [name of child] is sitting quietly and doing something that you like [name of child] to do?)

22. What assistance do you receive for you and your child? Who from? Was it easy to access services? Were your wishes taken into account?

23. Who do you discuss the needs of your child with? *(Probe for services and family members)*

24. How involved are the other children in the decision-making?

25. What other help do you receive? *(Probe for formal, semi-formal and informal sources of support)*

26. How do you feel about this support? *(Probe for benefits, problems and feelings of responsibility)* How has this support changed your life?

27. What else makes things easier for you? What sorts of things would help you now?

28. What concerns you most about your child at the moment? *(Probe for any problems or fears)*

29. How do you cope with any difficult times? Does it help?

30. What gives you the most happiness about your child?

31. How do you feel about your child's school? *(Probe for feelings about the school)*

32. What does he/she enjoy doing at school? What does he/she enjoy doing at home?

33. What advice would you give to another parent in a similar situation?

34. How do you see things in five years time? Ten years time?

35. Do you have any concerns about your child's future?

36. What are your dreams for the future of your child?

37. Is there anything else you would like to say? *(Also probe for opinions about the interview)*

Interview Schedules Used in the Phase 2 Interviews

Family information

These items summarise questions used in a study with 54 UK South Asian families with an adolescent/adult with learning disabilities (Hatton *et al.* 1998) and a cross-cultural survey of over 600 UK parents of a child with severe disabilities of Black African-Caribbean, Indian, Pakistani and Bangladeshi ethnic origin (Chamba *et al.* 1999):

10. Interviewee (main carer): age, gender, marital status, religion, ethnicity, disabilities, relationship to child with learning disabilities, number of years resident in UK, language fluency, preference and use.

11. Interviewee ethnic identity: two items concerning the extent to which interviewees identify themselves as Asian and/or British taken from the Policy Studies Institute 4th National Survey of Ethnic Minorities (Modood *et al.* 1997), a survey of 8063 UK adults across a range of ethnic groups.

12. Interviewee response bias due to social desirability effects (saying what the interviewee thinks the interviewer wants to hear); measured using the 10-item yes/no short version of the Marlowe-Crowne Social Desirability Scale (Strahan and Gerbasi 1972) used in previous research with UK families with a child with disabilities (Sloper *et al.* 1988; Sloper and Turner 1991, 1994).

13. Child with learning disabilities: age, gender, ethnicity, diagnosis.

14. Other people with disabilities in household: age, gender.

15. All people in the household: age, gender, relationship to child with learning disabilities, marital status, work status, place of birth.

Household information

Items and scales relating to household information were taken from Chamba *et al.* (1999):

1. Housing: home ownership, physical characteristics of home, sharing of home, suitability of home for looking after child with disabilities, alterations to home for child, length of time at current address, reasons for any recent house move.

2. Employment: employment status of interviewee and spouse/partner, effect of child on employment status and preference, difficulties in combining work and family.

3. Costs of looking after child with disabilities.

4. Income and benefits: household weekly income, receipt of benefits, income sent to other dependants outside the household.

Child characteristics

Items and scales relating to characteristics of the child with severe learning disabilities were taken from the Caregiver Information Questionnaire (CIQ) (Kozloff *et al.* 1994), a set of scales developed in the US to evaluate the success of educational interventions for children with developmental disabilities. This set of scales was the most concise method for assessing a number of constructs rated as important by parents in Phase 1 interviews.

1. Child traits: 15 items (scored on 4-point Likert scales) concerning a range of stable child characteristics, scored into four scales:

    (a) Acting out/aggressive (8 items);

    (b) Sad/withdrawn (2 items);

    (c) Happy/affectionate (3 items);

    (d) Co-operative (2 items).

2. Child functional skills: 24 items concerning a range of functional skills displayed by the child, scored into four scales:

    (a) Self-care skills (11 items);

    (b) Communication skills (4 items);

(c)   Interest in activities (5 items);

(d)   Social skills (4 items).

3.   Child problem behaviours: 12 items concerning the severity of a range of child problem behaviours, scored into one overall child problem behaviours scale.

4.   Child progress in past six months: 5 items concerning parent perceptions of the child's progress in the past six months scored into one overall child progress scale.

Social life

Information concerning the social life of the child and the family was gained using the Social Life Index, used in a study of 123 UK families with a child with Down's syndrome (Sloper *et al.* 1990):

1.   Family transport (access to a car, use of private and public transport).

2.   Parent social life and interests (length of time child can be left unsupervised, restrictions on parent social activities).

3.   Child social life – organisation: an index based on the range and frequency of the child's involvement in organised activities (for example special needs social club, mosque).

4.   Child social life – friends: an index based on the range and frequency of the child's involvement in social activities with friends (both with and without disabilities).

Disclosure

Information concerning the disclosure process was gained using the Index of Good Practice in Disclosure, developed in a UK study of parents of a child with severe physical disabilities (Sloper and Turner 1993). Additional items concerning language issues in disclosure were added for our study. This measure is scored to produce the following scales:

1.   The extent to which the disclosure was conducted in a professional manner.

2.   The quality of information provided at disclosure.

3.   Whether all criteria for good practice in disclosure had been met.

4.   The number of criteria for good practice in disclosure achieved.

Service support

Information was collected on several aspects of service support, drawing on a range of structured interview schedules. Information was grouped into the following areas of support from services:

1.   Awareness, frequency of use and rated helpfulness of 37 service supports in the past three months, using an adaptation of the Client Service Receipt Interview (Personal Social Services Research Unit 1990) used in previous research with UK South Asian families with an adolescent or adult with learning disabilities (Hatton *et al.* 1998).

2.   School: information concerning education services was drawn largely from previous surveys (Chamba *et al.* 1999; Hatton *et al.* 1998). Items concerned the nature of the education service, statements of special educational needs, aspects of the functioning of the education provision, whether education services meet the cultural and/or religious needs of the child.

3.   Keyworker: two questions from Chamba *et al.* (1999) concerning the use and perceived helpfulness of keyworkers.

4.   Respite/short-term care services: 16 items concerning awareness, use and helpfulness of respite/short-term care services were drawn from Chamba *et al.* (1999). Non-users of respite care were also asked why respite care was not used, and all interviewees were asked for ideas to improve respite care services.

5.   Experiences of professional interpreters: three checklists taken from Chamba *et al.* (1999).

6.   Parent groups: 2 items concerning the use and functions of parent support groups taken from Chamba *et al.* (1999).

7.   Informational support: 4 items concerning information needs and the preferred source of information, taken from Chamba *et al.* (1999).

8.   Problems with services: taken from Chamba *et al.* (1999), 17 yes/no items are asked concerning a range of potential problems with services, scored into four scales:

(a) Lack of confidence in professionals (6 items);

(b) Fight to get services (4 items);

(c) Inconvenient hospital services (3 items);

(d) Difficult communication with services (4 items).

9. Satisfaction with services and overall relationship with service professionals: 2 items taken from Chamba *et al.* (1999).

10. Future care: 4 items concerning parents' expectations of future support for the child with severe learning disabilities, taken from Chamba *et al.* (1999).

Informal support from family, friends and others

Information was gathered concerning various aspects of informal supports, taken from a variety of sources:

1. Receipt of practical and emotional support from a spouse or partner, support from other children in the household, and the availability and uptake of support from family members outside the household, taken from Chamba *et al.* (1999).

2. The Family Support Scale (Dunst *et al.* 1988), an 18-item measure of helpfulness to the family of different supports in the past three to six months, used in US research with families with a child with disabilities. For the purposes of this study, support items were divided into three sources; formal (5 items), semi-formal (3 items) and informal (10 items). For each of these sources of support, a total helpfulness score was computed across all relevant items. In addition, a mean helpfulness score was computed across relevant items where the interviewee had rated receiving some support, even if this support was unhelpful.

3. The Inventory of Social Support (Dunst *et al.* 1988), a 12-item measure developed with US families with a child with disabilities. This measure asks about which sources (from a choice of 19) provide 12 different types of support and assistance to the parent.

Family decision-making

A 9-item measure was developed for our study to investigate different aspects of family decision-making regarding the child with disabilities.

Family needs

A 32-item measure concerning the extent to which a range of family needs was met, taken from Chamba *et al.* (1999), scored into a total scale of unmet needs.

Parental coping

The 66-item Ways of Coping Questionnaire (Revised), previously used with 182 UK parents of a child with Down's syndrome (Knussen *et al.* 1992), was used for this study, scored into six scales for our study:

1. Acceptance/positive reappraisal (13 items).
2. Wishful thinking (9 items).
3. Practical coping (9 items).
4. Seeking social support (9 items).
5. Cognitive distraction (thinking about something else to take your mind off the problem) (7 items).
6. Behavioural distraction (doing something else to take your mind off the problem) (7 items).

Parental mental health

The following measures of parental mental health were used in our study:

1. General parental distress was assessed using the 24-item Malaise Inventory (Rutter *et al.* 1970), previously used in several UK studies of families with a child with disabilities (Kiernan and Alborz 1994; Sloper *et al.* 1988; Sloper and Turner 1991, 1994) and a UK survey of South Asian parents of an adolescent or adult with learning disabilities (Hatton *et al.* 1998). Total scores can be used, and can also be converted into threshold scores (six or above), where the person is thought to be at risk of psychological disorder.

2. Parental anxiety and depression were assessed using a translated and extensively validated version of the Clinical Interview Schedule (Lewis *et al.* 1992) as part of the 4th National Survey of 6081 UK adults across a range of ethnic groups (Nazroo 1998). Anxiety and depression scores and clinical threshold scores can be produced using the Clinical Interview Schedule.

Parental physical health

The 4th National Survey of 6081 UK adults across a range of ethnic groups included a section on physical health (Nazroo 1997). This section consisted of translated and validated health items from the Health Survey for England (White *et al.* 1993), with the 4th National Survey adding items drawn from a variety of sources (see Nazroo 1997 for details). Domains of physical health included:

1. Self-assessed health and activities limited by the respondent's health.

2. Cardiovascular disease.

3. Diabetes.

4. Respiratory symptoms.

5. Perceived weight.

6. Health-related behaviours such as smoking and drinking.

7. Accidents requiring medical treatment.

8. Use of health services and medication receipt.

Probe Questions for Phase 3 Interviews

1. What could services do to improve your understanding of your child's learning disability?

2. What do you feel would help you and your child the most on a typical bad day?

3. What do you think Asian carers need from services for a female/male child, and why?

4. What do you think is the impact of caring on brothers and/or sisters, and what could be done to help?

5. What would encourage you to use respite/short-term care for your child?

6. Would you make use of a drop-in centre, and what should it be like?

7. How have you received information about services and your child's disability?

8. In what language and form do you want to receive information?

9. Where do you think language support is most needed by Asian carers?

10. What information do you need for you and your child?

11. What recommendations would you make to improve disclosure?

12. What recommendations would you make to improve services now?

13. What would you like most from carer support groups, and should these groups be 'Asian' or 'mixed'?

14.   *(For children over 14).* What is the transition process like, and what major problems are you having about your child leaving school?

15.   What would be the ideal help from services for your child's future care?

16.   What is your greatest concern and need from adult day services?

17.   We found that a keyworker was associated with greater parental distress, depression and anxiety. Can you suggest any explanations?

18.   What do you think are the most important influences that make carers depressed or anxious?

19.   The least helpful service was stated as the social worker. Can you suggest why?

20.   Have you ever had any problems with the use of interpreters/Asian staff, and what improvements can be made?

21.   From the findings, what do you think of specifically Asian services for your child?

22.   How do you think we should improve the cultural/religious awareness of non-Asian staff?

23.   What do you believe to be the three most urgent improvements to services? How?

24.   What message would you like to give to the government?

References

Ahmad, W.I.U. and Atkin, K. (1996) (eds) *'Race' and Community Care.* Buckingham: Open University Press.

Atkin, K. and Rollings, J. (1996) 'Looking after their own? Family care-giving among Asian and Afro-Caribbean communities.' In W.I.U. Ahmad and K. Atkin (eds) *'Race' and Community Care.* Buckingham: Open University Press.

Azmi, S., Hatton, C., Emerson, E. and Caine, A. (1997) 'Listening to adolescents and adults with intellectual disabilities from South Asian communities.' *Journal of Applied Research in Intellectual Disabilities 10,* 3, 250–263.

Baldwin, S. and Carlisle, J. (1994) *Social Support for Disabled Children and their Families.* London: HMSO.

Baxter, C., Poonia, K., Ward, L. and Nadirshaw, Z. (1990) *Double Discrimination: Issues and Services for People with Learning Difficulties from Black and Minority Ethnic Communities.* London: King's Fund Centre.

Beresford, B. (1995) *Expert Opinions: A national survey of parents caring for a severely disabled child.* Bristol: The Policy Press.

Berry, J.W., Poortinga, Y.H., Segall, M.H. and Dasen, P.R. (2002) *Cross-Cultural Psychology: Research and applications (2nd edn).* Cambridge: Cambridge University Press.

Blacher, J. (2001) 'Transition to adulthood: mental retardation, families, and culture.' *American Journal on Mental Retardation 106,* 2, 173–188.

Chamba, R., Ahmad, W., Hirst, M., Lawton, D. and Beresford, B. (1999) *On The Edge: Minority Ethnic Families Caring For A Severely Disabled Child.* Bristol: The Policy Press.

Connors, C. and Stalker, K. (2003) *The Views and Experiences of Disabled Children and Their Siblings: A Positive Outlook.* London: Jessica Kingsley.

Department of Health (1998) *The Quality Protects Programme: Transforming Children's Services (LAC(98) 28).* London: Department of Health.

Department of Health (1999) *Caring About Carers: The Report of the National Carers Strategy.* London: The Stationery Office.

Department of Health (2001) *Valuing People: A New Strategy for Learning Disability for the 21st Century.* London: The Stationery Office.

Dunst, C.J., Trivette, C.M. and Deal, A.G. (1988) *Enabling and Empowering Families: Principles and Guidelines for Practice.* Cambridge, MA: Brookline.

Emerson, E. (2003) 'Mothers of children and adults with intellectual disability: social and economic situation, mental health status, and the self-assessed social and psychological impact of the child's difficulties.' *Journal of Intellectual Disability Research 47,* 4–5, 385–399.

Emerson, E., Azmi, S., Hatton, C., Caine, A., Parrott, R. and Wolstenholme, J. (1997) 'Is there an increased prevalence of severe learning disabilities among British Asians?' *Ethnicity and Health 2*, 4, 317–321.

Emerson, E. and Hatton, C. (1998) 'Residential provision for people with intellectual disabilities in England, Wales and Scotland.' *Journal of Applied Research in Intellectual Disabilities 11*, 1, 1–14.

Emerson, E. and Hatton, C. (1999) 'Future trends in the ethnic composition of British society and among British citizens with learning disabilities.' *Tizard Learning Disability Review 4*, 4, 28–32.

Emerson, E. and Hatton, C. (in press) Letter to the editor. *Journal of Intellectual Disability Research*.

Emerson, E., Hatton, C., Felce, D. and Murphy, G. (2001) *Learning Disabilities: The Fundamental Facts*. London: Foundation for People with Learning Disabilities.

Floyd, F.J., Singer, G.H.S., Powers, L.E. and Costigan, C.L. (1996) 'Families coping with mental retardation: assessment and therapy.' In J.W. Jacobson and J.A. Mulick (eds) *Manual of Diagnosis and Professional Practice in Mental Retardation*. Washington, DC: American Psychological Association.

Hatton, C. (2002) 'People with intellectual disabilities from ethnic minority communities in the US and the UK.' *International Review of Research in Mental Retardation 25*, 209–239.

Hatton, C. (in press) 'Cultural issues.' In E. Emerson, C. Hatton, T. Thompson and T. Parmenter (eds) *Handbook of Research Methods in Intellectual Disabilities*. Chichester: Wiley.

Hatton, C., Akram, Y., Shah, R., Robertson, J. and Emerson, E. (2002) *Supporting South Asian Families with a Child with Severe Disabilities: A report to the Department of Health*. Lancaster: Institute for Health Research, Lancaster University.

Hatton, C., Azmi, S., Caine, A. and Emerson, E. (1998) 'Informal carers of adolescents and adults with learning difficulties from the South Asian communities: family circumstances, service support and carer stress.' *British Journal of Social Work 28*, 6, 821–837.

Kerr, G. (2001) 'Assessing the needs of learning disabled young people with additional disabilities.' *Journal of Learning Disabilities 5*, 157–174.

Kiernan, C.C. and Alborz, A. (1994) *Factors Influencing the Ending of Informal Care for Adults with Learning Disabilities: Report to the Mental Health Foundation*. Manchester: Hester Adrian Research Centre, University of Manchester.

Knussen, C., Sloper, P., Cunningham, C.C. and Turner, S. (1992) 'The use of the Ways of Coping (Revised) Questionnaire with parents of children with Down's syndrome.' *Psychological Medicine 22*, 3, 775–786.

Kozloff, M.A., Cutler, B.C., Helm, D.T., Douglas-Steele, D. and Wells, A.I. (1994) 'Caregiver Information Questionnaire.' In M.A. Kozloff (ed) *Improving Educational Outcomes for Children with Disabilities: Guidelines and Protocols for Practice*. Baltimore: Paul H Brookes.

Laybourn, A. and Hill, M. (1991) *Children with Epilepsy and their Families: Needs and Services*. Glasgow: Central Research Unit Papers, Scottish Office, Department of Social Policy and Social Work, University of Glasgow.

Lewis, G., Pelosi, A.J., Araya, R. and Dunn, G. (1992) 'Measuring psychiatric disorder in the community: a standard assessment for use by lay interviewers.' *Psychological Medicine 22*, 2, 465–488.

McGrother, C.W., Bhaumik, S., Thorpe, C.F., Watson, J.M., and Taub, N.A. (2002) 'Prevalence, morbidity and service need among South Asian and white adults with intellectual disability in Leicestershire, UK.' *Journal of Intellectual Disability Research 46*, 299–309.

Mason, J. (1996) *Qualitative Researching.* London: Sage.

Mir, G., Nocon, A. and Ahmad, W. with Jones, L. (2001) *Learning Difficulties and Ethnicity.* London: Department of Health.

Modood, T., Berthoud, R., Lakey, J., Nazroo, J., Smith, P., Virdee, S. and Beishon, S. (1997) *Ethnic Minorities in Britain: Diversity and Disadvantage.* London: Policy Studies Institute.

Nazroo, J.Y. (1997) *The Health of Britain's Ethnic Minorities.* London: Policy Studies Institute.

Nazroo, J.Y. (1998) *Ethnicity and Mental Health: Findings from a National Community Survey.* London: Policy Studies Institute.

Newland, J. (1999) 'Assessing cultural identity in people with learning disabilities.' *Tizard Learning Disability Review 4*, 4, 20–24.

Office for National Statistics (2001) *Family Expenditure Survey 1999–2000.* London: Office for National Statistics.

Office for National Statistics (2003) Census 2001 Website. http://www.statistics.gov.uk/census2001

Owen, D. (1996) 'Size, structure and growth of the ethnic minority populations.' In D. Coleman and J. Salt (eds) *Ethnicity in the 1991 Census Volume One: Demographic characteristics of the ethnic minority populations.* London: HMSO.

Personal Social Services Research Unit (1990) *Client Service Receipt Interview.* Canterbury: Personal Social Services Research Unit, University of Kent.

Quinton, D. (2004) *Supporting Parents: Messages from Research.* London: Jessica Kingsley Publishers.

Ramcharan, P., Grant, G. and Flynn, M. (in press) 'Emancipatory and participatory research: how far have we come?' In E. Emerson, C. Hatton, T. Parmenter and T. Thompson (eds) *Handbook of Research in Intellectual Disabilities.* Chichester: Wiley.

Roberts, K. and Lawton, D. (1998) *Reaching Its Target? Disability living allowance for children: Social Policy Reports No 9.* York: Social Policy Research Unit, University of York.

Rutter, M., Tizard, J. and Whitmore, K. (1970) *Education, Health and Behaviour.* Harlow: Longman.

Seltzer, M.M., Floyd, F.J. and Hindes, A.R. (in press) 'Research methods in intellectual disabilities: the family context.' In E. Emerson, C. Hatton, T. Parmenter and T. Thompson (eds) *Handbook of Methods for Research and Evaluation in Intellectual Disabilities.* Chichester: Wiley.

Shah, R. (1995) *The Silent Minority: Children with Disabilities in Asian Families.* London: National Children's Bureau.

Shah, R. (1998) *Sharing The News: A Good Practice Guide and Training Pack for professionals working with Asian families when they are first told about their child's disability.* London: Mental Health Foundation.

Shah, R and Hatton, C. (1999) *Caring Alone: Young carers in South Asian communities.* London: Barnardo's.

Sloper, P., Cunningham, C.C., Knussen, C. and Turner, S. (1988) *A Study of the Process of Adaptation in a Cohort of Children with Down's Syndrome and their Families: Report to the Department of Health.* Manchester: Hester Adrian Research Centre, University of Manchester.

Sloper, P. and Turner, S. (1991) *Adaptation and Help-Seeking in Families of Children with Physical Disabilities: Report to the Department of Health.* Manchester: Hester Adrian Research Centre, University of Manchester.

Sloper, P. and Turner, S. (1993) 'Determinants of parental satisfaction with disclosure of disability.' *Developmental Medicine and Child Neurology 35,* 9, 816–825.

Sloper, P. and Turner, S. (1994) *Families of Teenagers with Down's Syndrome; Parent, Child and Sibling Adaptation: Report to the Economic and Social Research Council.* Manchester: Hester Adrian Research Centre, University of Manchester.

Sloper, P., Turner, S., Knussen, C. and Cunningham, C.C. (1990) 'Social life of school children with Down's syndrome.' *Child: Care, Health and Development 16,* 4, 235–251.

Smith, J.A. (1995) 'Semi-structured interviewing and qualitative analysis.' In J.A. Smith, R. Harre and L. Van Langenhove (eds) *Rethinking Methods in Psychology.* London: Sage.

Smith, J.A. (1996) 'Beyond the divide between cognition and discourse: using interpretative phenomenological analysis in health psychology.' *Psychology and Health 11,* 2, 261–271.

Smith, J.A., Jarman, M. and Osborn, M. (1999) 'Doing interpretative phenomenological analysis.' In M. Murray and K. Chamberlain (eds) *Qualitative Health Psychology: Theories and Methods.* London: Sage.

Strahan, R. and Gerbasi, K.C. (1972) 'Short homogenous versions of the Marlowe-Crowne Social Desirability Scale.' *Journal of Clinical Psychology 28,* 191–193.

Turner, S. and Sloper, P. (1992) 'Paediatricians' practice in disclosure and follow-up of severe physical disability in young children.' *Developmental Medicine and Child Neurology 34,* 4, 348–358.

White, A., Nicolaas, G., Foster, K., Browne, F. and Carey, S. (1993) *Health Survey for England 1991.* London: HMSO.

Subject Index

Author Index